Contemporary
British Architects

D0746687

DATE DUE

Royal Academy of Arts

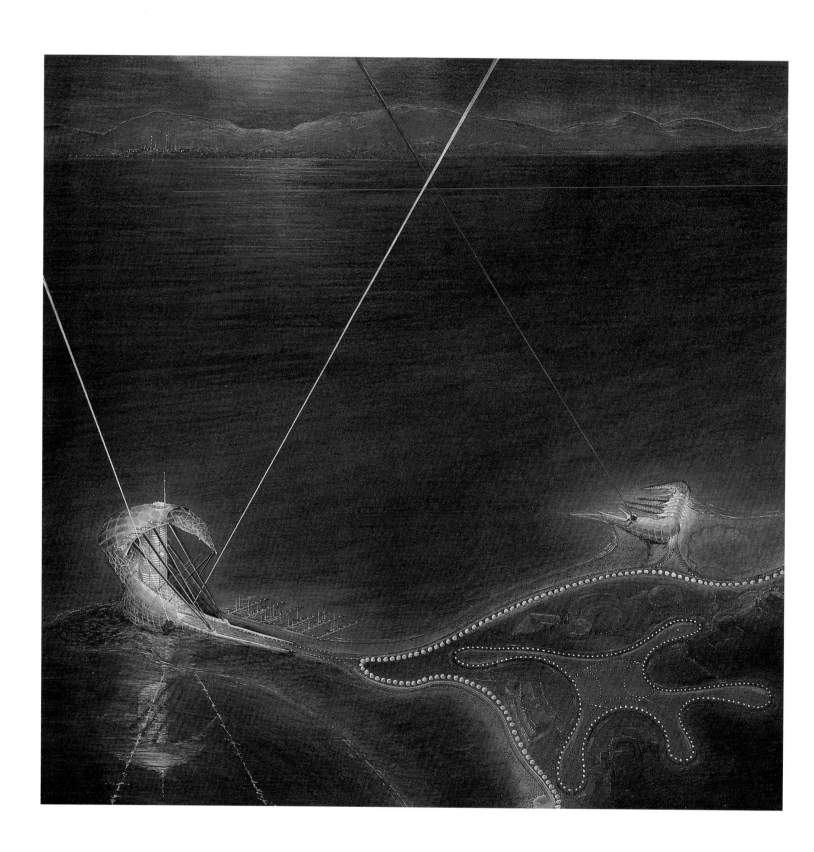

Contemporary British Architects

Recent Projects from the Architecture Room
of the Royal Academy Summer Exhibition

Essays by Peter Murray and Robert Maxwell

Royal Academy of Arts

Prestel, Munich and New York

First published to accompany the exhibition *Contemporary British Architects: Recent Projects from the Architecture Room of the Royal Academy Summer Exhibition*, organized by the Royal Academy of Arts, London, and shown in the United States at various venues between September 1994 and April 1996.

Cover 1:1,000 model of the Zoofenster building for Brau und Brunnen AG: view from Bahnhof Zoo station. Architects: Richard Rogers Partnership. Photo: Eamonn O'Mahony. (pp. 142/143)
Frontispiece Drawing in crayon and ink on film of Morecambe Seafront scheme (detail). Architects: Birds Portchmouth Russum. (pp. 42/43)

© Prestel-Verlag, Munich and New York, and Royal Academy of Arts, London, 1994

Prestel-Verlag
16 West 22nd Street, New York, NY 10010, USA
Phone (212) 627 8199, fax (212) 627 9866
and
Mandlstrasse 26, D-80802 Munich, Germany
Phone (89) 38 17 09 0, fax (89) 38 17 09 35

Distributed in continental Europe by Prestel-Verlag
Verlegerdienst München GmbH & Co. KG
Gutenbergstrasse 1, D-82205 Gilching, Germany
Phone (8105) 38 81 17, fax (8105) 38 81 00

Distributed in the USA and Canada on behalf of Prestel by
te Neues Publishing Company
16 West 22nd Street, New York, NY 10010, USA
Phone (212) 627 9090, fax (212) 627 9534

Distributed in Japan on behalf of Prestel by
YOHAN-Western Publications Distribution Agency
14-9 Okubo 3-chome, Shinjuku-ku, Tokyo 169, Japan
Phone (3) 32 08 01 81, fax (3) 32 09 02 88

Distributed in the United Kingdom, Ireland,
and all remaining countries on behalf of Prestel by
Thames & Hudson Limited
30-34 Bloomsbury Street,
London WC1B 3QP, England
Phone (71) 636 5488, fax (71) 636 1659

Exhibition curated by: Peter Murray and MaryAnne Stevens
Exhibition organiser and coordinating editor: Lucy Bullivant

Reproductions by Karl Dörfel Reproduktions GmbH, Munich
Printed by Aumüller Druck KG, Regensburg
Bound by MIB Conzella, Aschheim near Munich

Printed in Germany

ISBN 3-7913-1349-5 (Hardcover edition)

Contents

Foreword

Architecture has always played a central role in the life of the Royal Academy of Arts. Founded by Royal charter in 1768, the institution was as much the creation of Sir William Chambers, the distinguished neoclassical architect of Somerset House, London, and erstwhile tutor of architecture to King George III before he ascended the throne, as it was that of its first President, the painter Sir Joshua Reynolds. In its Instrument of Foundation, the Royal Academy was enjoined 'to promote the arts of design', and hence it rightly accorded architecture a position comparable to that of painting and sculpture, in its annual exhibition of contemporary art, which has been held without interruption since 1769.

This publication accompanies the exhibition *Contemporary British Architects*. It presents a selection of distinguished projects that have been shown by British architects, both members of the Royal Academy and others, in the Architecture Room of the annual summer exhibition since 1991. It draws on the stylistic diversity which distinguishes contemporary architecture and which is reflected in the scores of works shown in the Architecture Room in recent years. The exhibition, and hence this book, encompass work adhering to the principles of high technology and work informed by a profound regard for tradition. Some of the projects chosen have subsequently been realised, while others have remained as works on paper, created as entries for competitions, as manifestations of research or as independent works of art. The range of projects is reflected in the modes of presentation proffered by individual architects or practices, namely, from diagrammatic sketch, through working drawing and meticulously finished elevation, to architectural model. Equally significantly, the selection not only includes work by distinguished British architects of international repute but also presents designs by younger, often highly experimental practitioners in the fields of architecture, urban design, landscape architecture, and conservation.

The concept of this exhibition was initially sketched out by Sir Roger de Grey, Past President of the Royal Academy, and was given material form by its curator, Peter Murray, and by MaryAnne Stevens, Librarian and Head of Education at the Royal Academy. Together they also planned the accompanying publication, to which Peter Murray and Robert Maxwell have contributed important essays. The exhibition was organised and the publication further developed, expanded, and coordinated by Lucy Bullivant, Heinz Curator of Architectural Programmes at the Royal Academy, with able research assistance from Diana Hunt, Philippa Thomas, and Catherine Levy, and administrative assistance from Freda Matassa and members of the Royal Academy's Exhibitions Office. The book would not have been realised without the invaluable collaborative efforts of Andrea P.A. Belloli at Prestel-Verlag and editor Stephanie Salomon.

In presenting in the United States a cross section of excellent contemporary British architecture, this exhibition demonstrates both the Royal Academy's continuing commitment to architecture and its vital relationship with that country. We are delighted to acknowledge the sustained support of Katherine Ockenden of the American Associates of the Royal Academy Trust.

Architecture is not merely about bricks and mortar, nor about glass and steel. It makes a statement about a society's values, and living space, and what it projects as an expression of its own culture. To design with a respect for the past, to build an acceptable present, and to project a vision for the future are challenges that have always confronted the architect. That this exhibition seeks to demonstrate the vitality and variety of responses to such a challenge is to testify to the inventiveness and excellence present in British architecture today.

Sir Philip Dowson
President
Royal Academy of Arts

Peter Murray

A catholic assembly: architecture and the Academy

Historical background: the Academy's engagement with architecture

The Royal Academy of Arts has from its foundation in 1768 celebrated all the plastic arts - painting, sculpture, engraving and the mother of them all, architecture. A letter sent to King George III on 28 November 1768 reads: "May it please your Majesty, We, your Majesty's most faithful subjects, Painters, Sculptors, and Architects of this metropolis, being desirous of establishing a Society for promoting the Arts of Designs... most humbly beg leave to solicit your Majesty's gracious assistance, patronage and protection". George III speedily agreed to provide the necessary support, and the Academy was set up the following month.

Among the twenty-two signatories of this letter was Sir William Chambers, one of the most distinguished architects of the 18th century. At the age of 33 years he had been appointed architectural tutor to the heir to the throne, the Prince of Wales; finding favour at court, he rose to the prestigious position of Architect of the King's Works. Concerned that artists in Britain should be represented by a professional body, Chambers was a prime mover in the establishment in 1763 of the Society of Arts; five year later his dissatisfaction with this institution caused him to lead a breakaway group which ultimately constituted the founding members of the Royal Academy of Arts. Through his privileged position at Court, Chambers not only obtained George III's agreement to accord royal status to the nascent Academy but also to underwrite its financial survival at least for the first three years of its existence. To ensure that its finances were competently handled, the King, however, insisted that Chambers be appointed the Academy's first Treasurer in order that he "may have a person in whom he places full confidence, in an office where his interest is concerned". Chambers took good care of the King's investment. Joshua Reynolds, the first President of the Academy, described Chambers as the "Vice-roy" over him; all the major business with the Sovereign was conducted through the Treasurer. The appointment of Chambers set a precedent, and for the next 110 years the Treasurers of the Academy were all architects and appointed for life – presumably because it was thought that architects had a better head for figures than other artists. Since 1880, while the position of Treasurer has continued to be the prime domain of architectural members, they have been elected to that office for limited terms.

The Academy's Instrument of Foundation of 1768 outlined the constitution and activities of the organisation. One of its three founding obligations was the establishment of a school under the direction of the "ablest artists". Among the professorships to be filled – in Painting, Anatomy, Perspective, and Ancient History - was that of Architecture. The obligation of this position was to "read annually six public lectures, calculated to form the taste of the students, to instruct them in the laws and principles of composition". This provided the first professional teaching of architecture in England outside the traditional apprenticeship system.

The first Professor of Architecture was Thomas Sandby. Although he built little, he was important as a pioneer of perspective drawing. He delivered his first six lectures (copies of his texts survive in the libraries of the Royal Institute of British Architects, the Royal Academy and the Sir John Soane's Museum) in 1770, and repeated them annually until his death in 1789. One of his most influential designs, which accompanied his sixth lecture, was for a 'Bridge of Magnificence' across the River Thames. This caused something of a stir when it was exhibited in the Annual Exhibition of 1781; such accomplished and dramatic perspectives of architectural designs scarcely had been seen before in England. A colonnade of Doric columns stretches from one bank of the river to the other; domed wings at each end contain apartments. The work was undoubtedly influenced by the triumphal bridges designed by Piranesi some years earlier in Italy. Sandby's designs in turn influenced the young John Soane, who recalled the powerful impression which the sight of that "beautiful work produced on myself and many of the young Artists of those days". Soane designed a bridge of his own, winning the Academy Schools Gold Medal and a

Richard Earlom, The Exhibition of the Royal Academy, 1771, in its Room in Pall Mall. Mezzotint from a watercolour by Charles Brandon. Royal Academy of Arts, London.

Charles Robert Cockerell, The Professor's Dream, exhibited at the Royal Academy in 1849. Watercolour. Royal Academy of Arts, London

travelling sholarship to Italy. Soane became Professor of Architecture in 1806 and drew six versions of his own Triumphal Bridge; creating variations of this design was a regular exercise for his students.

The Instrument of Foundation also decreed that 'there shall be an annual exhibition of paintings, sculptures and designs. All academicians, until they have attained the age of sixty, shall be obliged to exhibit at least one performance, under a penalty of five pounds'. At the first show, George Dance failed to exhibit and duly paid his fine. Dance was the architect of the now demolished Newgate Prison, one of the most dramatic buildings of its time in England. His omission clearly did not jeopardise his position at the Academy, and he became the second Professor of Architecture upon Sandby's death in 1789. Today the Academy is less strict, and Academicians are required to exhibit at least once every five years.

For the first eleven years of its life the Academy Annual Exhibition was held in modest premises in Pall Mall, but in 1780 the Academy moved to new quarters in Somerset House, which was designed by William Chambers to accommodate a number of Government Departments around three sides of a grand courtyard. The north side of the square was intended for various institutions, including the Academy, the Royal Society, and the Society of Antiquaries. In these new, larger rooms overlooking the Strand, the Annual Exhibition continued to grow in popularity. From 1795 onwards architectural design drawings were given a dedicated area within the exhibition. This is the earliest instance anywhere in Europe of an architectural exhibition *per se*. Elsewhere the policy was to show design drawings interspersed among other art forms. Despite the extra space, the paintings and perspectives were packed from floor to ceiling.

The Academy remained in Somerset House for just over fifty years before moving in 1837 into the east wing of the newly completed National Gallery in Trafalgar Square, designed by the Academician William Wilkins. Wilkins was made Professor of Architecture in the same year. These new quarters allowed

Pietro Antonio Martini, The Exhibition of the Royal Academy at Somerset House, 1787, after John Henry Ramberg. Line engraving. Royal Academy of Arts, London.

John Wykeham Archer, South Front, Burlington House, 1855. Watercolour. The Trustees of the British Museum, London

T E Collcutt, New Theatre, Cambridge Circus, for R D'Oyly Carte, Esq.,1865. Pen wash drawing. British Architectural Library, Royal Institute of British Architects Drawings Collection, London

the Annual Exhibition to grow, and in 1846 over fifteen hundred works were exhibited. In 1850, however, the Academy was informed that the National Gallery needed the space in the east wing. Alternative accommodations were sought, and, after considerable negotiation, the Government granted the Academy in 1866 a nine-hundred-and-ninety-nine-year lease at a rent of one pound per annum on Burlington House in Piccadilly. Sydney Smirke, who had held the Professorship of Architecture since 1861, was commissioned to alter the building to suit the Academy's needs, which he did by constructing the main galleries on the site of the garden and building on an extra floor that conformed to the height of the buildings on either side of the entrance courtyard.

The first Annual Exhibition in Smirke's new galleries at Burlington House was held in 1869; it included 1,320 works. This was fewer than had been hung in the National Gallery quarters despite the additional space, since it had been decided that 'every picture should be hung with its base not higher than 12 ft. from the ground because of criticisms from artists whose work had been 'skied,' that is, hung so high that it could hardly be seen. During the latter part of the nineteenth century the Annual Exhibition reached the peak of its popularity. In 1869 it received an amazing 315,000 visitors, that number growing in 1879 to 391,197. In 1993 the exhibition was seen by 120,000 visitors.

William Powell Frith, A Private View, 1881. © Pope Family Trust. Oil on canvas. The Bridgeman Art Library, London.

After the relatively inept presidency of the architect, James Wyatt, at the beginning of the 19th century, no architect was elected to this office until Aston Webb, in 1919. The designer of numerous national monuments, including the eastern facade of Buckingham Palace, Admiralty Arch and the southern facade of the Victoria and Albert Museum, South Kensington, Webb held the post of president until 1924, when serious injury incurred in an automobile accident on his return from the Academy Annual Dinner forced him to resign.

Fourteen years later another architect Edwin Lutyens – one of the most influential twentieth-century British architects – became President. Lutyens presided during the Second World War, which severely curtailed the Academy's activities. He did, however, set up the Royal Academy Planning Committee, the aim of which was to 'draw attention to the advantages that may be obtained by replanning on imaginative lines and to initiate a long-term policy of public benefit'. In 1942 the Committee of eminent architect-Academicians presented a 'plan for London's material, social and aesthetic requirements as conceived by architects, to solve some of the major problems of design; and, in general to state the case for an architectural approach to a great opportunity'. It produced a publication, *London Replanned*, in which it put forward a series of projects for rebuilding importants districts, such as Piccadilly Circus and the area surrounding Saint Paul's Cathedral, in the wake of the German blitzkrieg of central London. The urban design was classical in inspiration, with buildings set within formal layouts and grand vistas. The propos-

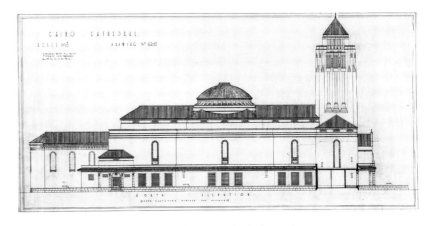

A. Gilbert Scott, North elevation of Cairo Cathedral, c. 1926. Pencil drawing on linen. British Architectural Library, Royal Institute of British Architects Drawings Collection, London

als aroused considerable contemporary interest, since they reflected the view generally held among architects that the bombing provided a great opportunity to replan London in a modern manner. In 1944 the Royal Academy Planning Committee published *Road, Rail and River in London*, which studied the capital's transportation needs. Few of the Academy's ideas were taken up, however, when the war ended.

In 1954 Albert Richardson, an architect of the anti-modernist school, was elected President of the Academy. He would describe multistorey flats as 'breeding boxes' and 'maggotries full of pale and squirming people'. In the late 1950s and early 1960s he epitomised stuffy conservatism to the postwar generation of students brought up on the principles of the International Style of Le Corbusier and the Bauhaus, disseminated by such schools of architecture as the Architectural Association. Anti-Ugly campaigners, a group of student and radical architects who protested against the tedium of much classically inspired postwar building, voted Richardson's *Financial Times* building the ugliest in the country. Richardson was Professor of Architecture at London University for twenty-five years; in 1946 he became Royal Academy Professor of Architecture, the first to be apointed since 1911. After temporary closure during World War II, a postgraduate architectural course was established by Richardson; it later survived somewhat hesitantly until 1957. Five years later, Basil Spence, the architect of Coventry Cathedral, was elected Professor of Architecture. Spence tackled the issue of architecture education within the Academy by attempting to organise an evening school in which students would be taught by distinguished visiting lecturers. However, this failed to attract postgraduates in sufficient numbers and was closed in 1964. Lectures under the auspices of the Professor of Architecture continued until 1968. Thus, for 200

J D M Harvey, Saint Paul's from the South, from the front cover of 'London Replanned', supplement to *Country Life, October 1942 issue*. Pencil drawing. Royal Academy of Arts, London.

View of the Sackler Galleries at the Royal Academy of Arts, designed by Sir Norman Foster and Partners, showing the Hokusai prints exhibition, 1991. *Photo: Dennis Gilbert*

Norman Foster, these galleries which present a discreet contemporary architecture of steel, glass, and white walls, which elegantly harmonise with their eighteenth- and nineteenth-century neighbours.

The Academy continues its historic engagement with, and support of architecture. In June 1993, a substantial endowment from the Heinz Foundation has enabled it to consolidate its programme of architectural exhibitions and educational events, including a prestigious international annual architecture lecture. It now looks forward to the realisation of plans to expand its operations into the Museum of Mankind, a grand mid-19th-century building by James Pennethorne which stands behind Burlington House. It is here that the Academy wishes to establish an architecture centre where it can develop its role in stimulating public interest in architectural ideas, issues and projects. In December 1993 Philip Dowson was elected President, the sixth architect to be so honoured. One of his main tasks will be to oversee these developments.

years, apart from breaks during the World War years, there was architectural teaching at the Royal Academy. In 1976 Hugh Casson was elected President. Casson had been knighted for his work on the Festival of Britain in 1951, ran a successful architectural practice, and was Professor of Environmental Design at the Royal College of Art. The presidency of his successor, the painter Roger de Grey, saw no falling off in the Academy's concern for architecture. The Academy organised a major exhibition, *New Architecture: Foster Rogers Stirling*, and it commissioned and built the new Sackler Galleries. Designed by the Academician,

Architecture and the Academy today

The influence of the Academy on the presentation of architecture in Britain at the end of the twentieth century may well be as great as it was in the latter part of the eighteenth century. The development of the perspective drawing of architectural subjects in eighteenth-century England can be attributed to the desire

Joseph Gandy ARA, Sketch for a new Senate House, exhibited 1835. Watercolour. British Architectural Library, Royal Institute of British Architects Drawings Collection, London

Sir Edwin L. Lutyens, Memorial to the Missing at Thiepval, begun 1923, completed 1930. Pencil and red crayon on headed notepaper. British Architectural Library, Royal Institute of British Architects Drawings Collection, London

Sir Edwin Cooper, Entrance corridor, Lloyds, London.
Pen and watercolour sketch, reproduced in volume 62
of *Academy Architecture*, 1931.

among architect Academicians to show images in the Annual Exhibition that could equal the visual impact of paintings and engravings. Perspectives constituted the most popular form of rendering in the Annual Exhibition as late as the early 1970s, when architects increasingly replaced them with simpler line drawings and models.

The Annual Exhibitions provide a fascinating cross section of the kinds of work architects were carrying out at any given time. In 1907, for example, when the British Empire was in its heyday and wealth from its colonies was pouring into the country, the exhibition included proposals for churches, school buildings, city halls, museums, public libraries, public baths, and office buildings designed in the Edwardian baroque style. In 1924, after the First World War, Reginald Blomfield exhibited his designs for a war memorial at the Menin Gate in Belgium, and Edwin Lutyens his eloquent Memorial to the Missing of the Somme at Thiepval in Northern France. There were also hospitals and offices and even Lutyens's facade for Queen Mary's dolls' house. By 1937 buildings housing telephone exchange equipment were reaching a level of architectural sophistication suitable for display in the Academy. In 1942 Edwin Cooper showed a "church proposed to be built postwar."

During the 1960s and 1970s the architectural offerings in the Annual Exhibition declined into a rather uninspiring mix of conservative tendencies and modernist presentations. In 1983 in the *Financial Times*, the architectural correspondent Colin Amery was prompted to write under the headline 'The Mediocre Curiosity Shop': "Every year it is harder and harder to imagine why any architect worth his salt bothers to show at the Royal Academy. At a time when any student show in almost any school of architecture can produce beautiful drawings it is almost incredible that some of the ancient, and not so ancient, leaders of the profession can get away with some of the rubbishy presentations that are to be seen on the walls of Burlington House."

By 1992, however, Amery had changed his mind: "Reviewing the Royal Academy's annual Summer Exhibition is one of the benchmarks for a critic of the architectural year. At the same time when the rate of new commissions for architects has slowed down alarmingly because of the recession, the RA provides a good opportunity to consider the state of the art". Even the more acerbic and modernist critic Deyan Sudjic took a positive view in *The Guardian* in 1993: "The architecture room has become the place to find out what is happening in architecture. Much of the felt pen and airbrush kitsch that used to dominate has disappeared as would-be exhibitors have become embarrassed by rising standards. Nor is the exhibition identified with any one architectural faction."

This change in perception is due partly to alterations in the layout of the Summer Exhibition. Until 1984 the architectural exhibits were dispersed throug-

The Architecture Room at the Royal Academy of Arts's annual Summer Exhibition presents a diverse range of projects in a variety of media. *Photo: Peter Murray*

Model and photographs of the Staatsgalerie, Stuttgart (1985), designed by James Stirling Michael Wilford and Partners, and shown as part of the exhibition 'New Architecture: Foster Rogers Stirling', Royal Academy of Arts, 1986. *Photo: Andy Weiner*

hout the galleries and thus tended to be overshadowed by painting and sculpture. In that year the architect Academicians were finally accorded a dedicated gallery in the centre of the building on the main axis. Almost contemporaneously architects were becoming more conscious of the need to present their work outside the profession, a practice which is facilitated by changes in the RIBA Code of Professional Conduct in the late 1970s. This meant that for the first time architects were able legally to promote themselves and their work. This has led to an improvement in the general quality of information prepared by architects for presentation on the gallery's walls.

The Academy contributed further to the public's appreciation of contemporary architecture when it organised in 1986 the most successful architectural exhibition ever held in Britain. More than one hundred thousand people viewed *The New Architecture: Foster Rogers Stirling*, which filled the Main Galleries of the Academy. All three architects were members of the Academy and each one showed two works: a project and a completed building. Richard Rogers included a detailed model and explanation of his shining, stainless steel building for Lloyd's, with its service cores positioned on the outside of the structure, allowing large uninterrupted floor areas within. A model of the Thames, an inky black tank of water, stretched from one end of a gallery to the other; and a silver suspension bridge carried pedestrians to an artificial island built in the middle of the 'river'. The bridge was part of a larger project by Rogers to improve the area between Leicester Square and the

South Bank by pedestrianisation, and by covering over the roadways and creating landscaped parks above them. James Stirling showed a dramatic full-size section of his Staatsgalerie in Stuttgart as well as his entry in the controversial competition for an extension to the National Gallery (which had been won by American architects Robert Venturi and Denise Scott Brown). Norman Foster used multi-screens and large-scale models to recreate his Hongkong and Shanghai Banking Corporation headquarters; he also offered his aborted designs for a new headquarters for the British Broadcasting Corporation. The BBC had recently cancelled the project in a cost-cutting exercise and commissioned instead a far less distinguished office block, much to the chagrin of those who had hoped that Foster would at last erect a major building in London. The exhibition, supported by substantial press coverage and public interest, celebrated the excellence of contemporary "modern architecture" and created a counterbalance to the call for a return to traditional architectural styles then being advocated by the Prince of Wales.

Balance is one of the most important contributions of the Architecture Room in the Annual Exhibition. Its eclectic selection mirrors the growing acceptance of pluralism during the past decade. High-tech sits side by side with classical revival, postmodernism coexists with deconstructivism, refurbishment with new build. The shows of the last three years have included a comprehensive cross-section of architects currently practising in Britain, from Robert Adam — who believes that classicism is an evolving style that is changed by developments in technology and use — to Quinlan Terry — a fundamentalist to whom the immutability of the classical tradition is paramount. Terry's exquisite elevations, generally of a new country house for a new country gentleman, have made regular appearances at the Annual Exhibition for the past twenty years.

Also featured are elaborate renderings of historic buildings. The significant amount of work related to the refurbishment of old buildings provides opportunities for architects to display their skills in measured drawings. Donald Insall, one of Britain's leading practitioners in the conservation of older buildings — responsible for such major projects as the restoration of the debating chamber of the House of Lords — regularly contributes a highly individual rendering that includes a collage of sections, plans, and calligraphed explanation. Robert Chitham, of Chapman Taylor Partners, is a master of the measured drawing and the pencil — a disappearing skill in the days of computer drafting.

Richard Rogers is at the other end of the architectural spectrum. His Meccano model of the K1 Tower

Model of Richard Rogers's speculative Silver Mile scheme which proposed a new pedestrian bridge across the River Thames, on display in the exhibition, 'New Architecture: Foster Rogers Stirling', Royal Academy of Arts, London, 1986. *Photo: Andy Weiner*

Exhibition Space in Tokyo has little in common, except for the quality of the architecture, with the gilt and gesso of the Government Offices designed by Sir George Gilbert Scott in 1862 and now being refurbished by the Cecil Denny Highton Group. Although Rogers is in the process of completing his second major building in London–the Channel 4 Building–much of his work, like that of Foster and Stirling, is outside Britain, such as his design for a new city on the outskirts of Shanghai.

Rogers and Foster are the senior members of the English 'school' of high-tech design, which in recent years has had a substantial representation at the Academy. Future Systems (Amanda Levete and Jan Kaplicky) is an experimental practice whose work pushes the relationship of architecture and technology to the extreme. Kaplicky has worked on designs for space stations with the National Aeronautics and Space Administration (NASA) in the United States, and his architecture reflects this background in terrestrial form. The use of lightweight materials, minimal ground connections, aerodynamic shapes, gaskets, and lunar-module feet all help to create an architecture of great optimism and excitement.

Richard Horden shares the ideals of Future Systems; however, his inspiration is the technology of yachts and sailing rather than that of outer space. Every beam is shaved to its most elegant and efficient cross-section, and each material chosen is the most lightweight possible. Out of such a dedicated response to the effects of natural forces comes an architecture of great beauty and refinement.

Although the fortunes of the marketplace have on the whole reserved Eva Jiricna's high-tech designs for the interiors of apartments and shops, she has turned the design of interior elements, particularly stairs, into an art form. Her shop for Joseph in Sloane Street, London (1992), like many of her other designs, focuses on a grand stair with intricate glass treads and stainless steel supports, which is both a beautiful and efficient structure.

Nicholas Grimshaw's work, on the other hand, occurs on an imposing scale. His design for the new Channel Tunnel terminal at Waterloo Station is on the scale of the great railway stations of the nineteenth century. The lofty arches, filigree structure, and complex arrangement of glazing all announce the debt high-tech design owes to the great Victorian engineers, particularly Joseph Paxton, the designer of the Crystal Palace, built for the Great Exhibition in 1851.

Michael Hopkins, known for projects such as the Schlumberger Building in Cambridge (1985), is associated with high-tech, but he has also earned the sobriquet of "the acceptable face of modernism" because of his skill in relating new, modern buildings to existing fabric. His most recent, and most challenging, project in this vein is at Glyndebourne. This small and fashionable opera house is part of an historic country house set in the depths of the Sussex countryside; its existing building was inadequate and

Hopkins was commissioned to increase its capacity and to improve its backstage facilities. The architect accomplished this by incorporating a mixture of contemporary features–such as the exposed structure of the fly tower–and the imaginative use of traditional materials.

Even though high-tech is often considered the foremost contemporary British style, there is perhaps a more naturally English school, one that the *Architectural Review* dubbed the 'romantic pragmatists'. Adherents are descendants of the nineteenth-century Arts and Crafts movement, rather than of engineers, and have been influenced by architects such as Richard Norman Shaw and Charles Voysey in Britain and Frank Lloyd Wright in the United States. Their work has a strong basis in building construction, and decoration and variety is created through the arrangement and juxtaposition of structure and materials. MacCormac Jamieson Prichard falls into this camp; the practice is best known for their university buildings in Oxford and Cambridge, which integrate sensible plans, timeless materials, and confident contextualism. Edward Cullinan illustrates a similar approach in his Fountains Abbey Visitor Centre in Yorkshire (1993), in which he assertively mixes traditional drystone walling with a contemporary curved roof. The centre, commissioned by the National Trust, is situated within a highly sensitive piece of landscape, yet it does not attempt to ape traditional structures or to copy the styles of buildings nearby.

The Academy encompasses two generations of architects inspired by the heroes of the modern movement – Le Corbusier, Gropius, Mies van der Rohe, and Mendelsohn. The older generation, once the radical avant-garde, is now well ensconced within the Establishment. Architectural practices such as HKPA Architects and Powell Moya & Partners made their reputations during the public building boom of the 1960s and 1970s (when Britain was erecting public housing, schools, universities and hospitals). Arup Associates also became known during this era but was one of the few of this group to respond to the changing economic climate of the 1980s and to build successfully for the commercial sector. Their buildings at Broadgate (1985–88) showed how sensitive architecture and speculative development could produce a first-class environment.

The new generation of modernists, which started to practice in the late 1970s and 1980s, has eschewed high-tech yet has survived the roller coaster of postmodernism. It is typified by practices such as Troughton McAslan, whose love affair with white and with clean, open space punctuated by fine materials and strong geometric features contains references to Le Corbusier and Mies van der Rohe, yet he rejects the "form follows function" school of modernism while embracing architecture as a means of creating form, space, and style. This mannerist modern movement is also represented by the work of Armstrong Architects, which has the distinction of most recently winning one of the competitions for the series of Grands Projets in Paris with its design for the Maison de la Culture du Japon.

The example of the French Government as a patron of architecture has in recent years put Britain to shame. It became unusual in the Thatcher era for buildings designed by public authorities to be noted for their architectural quality, and few examples are represented in the Academy's Architecture Room. The Hampshire County Architects Department is an exception. Its chief architect, Colin Stansfield Smith, was awarded the Royal Institute of British Architects Gold Medal by the RIBA in 1991 in recognition of his contribution to contemporary architecture. The department's reputation rests both on commissioning first-class outside architects and on generating high-quality designs by its own members.

There are some architects who fit into no category, who form no school, and whose highly individual works are rarely successfully imitated: James Stirling was such an architect. He varied his style several times in his career and was reaching a mature phase when the world of architecture was robbed of his genius by his untimely death in 1993. His early work, such as the Engineering Building at Leicester University (1963) and the History Faculty Library at Cambridge (1968), represented a new expressionism in modern architecture that owed as much to Victorian industrial and warehouse architecture as it did to the modern movement. His reliance on history and reference grew, reaching its apotheosis in his masterwork, the Staatsgalerie in Stuttgart (1984), which combined monumentality with a sympathetic consideration of the site, formal spaces with visual jokes, and details plucked straight from other architects' buildings with feats of daring originality. The Architecture Room of the 1993 Summer Show included a poignant tribute to Stirling's memory and contained a selection of early works as well as more recent ones.

The Academy's Annual Exhibition illustrates an encouraging view of the richness and diversity of talent to be found in contemporary British architecture, largely because it encompasses projects as well as built works. The volume of new building in Britain in these first years of the 1990s is small, the volume of excellent buildings very small indeed. Many of the leading architects are finding most of their work overseas: Grimshaw and Foster in Germany, Stirling (now Michael Wilford & Partners) in Singapore, Terry Farrell in Hong Kong. The later nineties might, how-

ever, provide a windfall for the Architecture Room;
the British Government lottery, slated to begin in
1995, will divert substantial funds towards the construction of buildings to mark the Millennium. Already projects such as a new Museum of Modern Art
have been proposed by the Tate Gallery, and the
South Bank Arts complex is working on plans for
major alterations to its galleries and concert halls.
Many of these projects will be the subject of competitions, thus creating a whole series of contributions to
the architectural debate.

The Millennium projects will also be highly public and thus will raise a number of issues about the
presentation of architecture to the non-specialist audience. The sumptuous drawings of Joseph Gandy and
William Walcot, which appeared in the Architecture
Rooms of past centuries were easily appreciated by
the layperson; the no less complex messages presented by many modern buildings have yet to find the
ideal presentation method. Models work well in
communicating the way a building works; plans and
sections are often essential but can be difficult to un-
derstand. While there is a feeling that presentations in
an art gallery should involve some aspect of the human hand, today more and more architectural drawings are created by computer. Computers can render
perspectives more accurately than artists – overcom-
ing criticisms made of perspectivists, particularly
those representing speculative developers in the
1960s and 1970s, who were seen as glossing over the
less attractive features of a design. The animated
computer rendering of a building is the most advanced method of presenting a design and offers the
greatest potential for communicating the real character of a project to a general audience. Perhaps we will
see in the year 2000 a Summer Show full of grand
Millennium schemes, as grand and adventurous as
Thomas Sandby's Bridge of Magnificence, but portrayed on monitors that allow the visitor to walk
through the building while controlling his own journey through the interactive system. If the Academy
hanging committee will in the future accept the video
monitor and the virtual reality helmet (it was only
seventy years ago that photographs were permitted

Thomas Sandby, A Bridge of Magnificence, c. 1760. Perspective
drawing in pen and wash on paper. British Architectural Library,
Royal Institute of British Architects Drawings Collection, London.

in the Annual Exhibition, three-quarters of a century
after Fox Talbot invented the negative process), let us
hope it will still include the finely drawn pencil perspective, the measured drawing, and the classical
woodcut.

It is the ability of the Annual Exhibition to contain variety that is its strength. This is particularly so
today when pluralism is viewed with approval by
the public and the professional. No other regular architectural exhibition in Britain exists that attempts
to present this cross section of talent. The Royal
Academy now hopes to take its involvement with
architecture one step further by setting up a permanent centre where it may take an even more active
role in what is becoming an increasingly public
debate.

Author's Note
For further information, the reader is referred to the following,
publications: Hutchison, Sidney C., The History of the Royal
Academy 1768–1986. Second ed. London: Chapman & Hall,
1986.
Lever, Jill, and Margaret Richardson. Art of the Architect.
London: Trefoil, 1984.
Stamp, Gavin. The Great Perspectivists. London: Trefoil, 1982.

Robert Maxwell

Architecture as art: transatlantic parallels

It would not be appropriate here to try to equal the insights of de Tocqueville on the differences between the American and the European character. The American nation of which he wrote was made up of ex-Europeans, and the differences he observed were produced by the challenges attendant on the project of bringing European civilisation to a vast and raw continent. Today, the United States of America is an advanced and populous nation of many diverse strains, a model perhaps for a multi-ethnic society of the future. The original British connection is just one of a multitude of influences that now combine to produce a rich and many-faceted society. If we are concerned here with the reinterpretation of British architecture to an American audience, it is precisely because of the changing circumstances that have reduced the British connection from the principal one – the Revolutionary War – to just one more case of specific ties and common interests, which may still be important for some Americans in their search for roots and origins, or of interest to both American and British natives in measuring the distances that each nation has travelled into new territory.

Eleven years of living and working in the United States have allowed me to see more clearly some of the differences, as well as many of the similarities, between the two countries, particularly in attitudes towards architects and architecture. There is a solid core of overlap, of common expectations, which is probably most clearly expressed in the Anglo-American empirical tradition in the fields of philosophy and science. The Ivy League universities are a repository of shared traditions and allegiances, even to agreement on the proper look of a university: Ralph Cram, the principal architect of Princeton University's campus, was sent to look at England's Oxford and Cambridge University quadrangles before preparing his designs. Yet, day to day, the British resident experiences a different culture. In the practice of architecture, even the basic vocabulary is different. The young British student arriving in the United States learns very quickly that a set-square is a triangle, a trim an architrave, a lavatory a washbasin, and a watercloset a lavatory.

In the United States, the career of architect is not looked down upon: if one's son or daughter elects to pursue studies in architecture, this is not cause for panic. There are two obvious reasons for this. First, professional training in the United States is for the most part conducted as part of a postgraduate education, followed by an internship. Entrance into a course of architectural training almost always requires a liberal arts degree (the undergraduate bachelor's degree). Thus architecture is not initially a technical subject of study, but a cultural one, frequently linked to the study of art history. One useful by-product of this arrangement is that not only are most architects well-educated in the liberal sense before they take up a professional career, but also a considerable number of educated people in society at large – who do not go on to become architects – know about architecture and are potentially enlightened clients. Second, architects are expected to be technically competent, but not to be mere technicians, still less to follow the exacting discipline of the sciences. They are expected to be able to instill concepts into their designs, to put forward an architecture that is equal to the other arts in terms of the ideas it incorporates and in terms of its intrinsic interest as a cultural contribution.

In Britain, on the other hand, the educational system is not designed to postpone career decisions but to advance them. The high school student must decide on a career direction before entering the last two years of study and must then select the examination track to be followed (that is, choose the subjects to take at Advanced level), which determines university entrance. Having embarked upon a five-year architecture course at university, it is very difficult to change one's subject, and the onus is on the student to prove competence, not artistic or scholarly intent. Architecture schools are usually linked to engineering, management, or social science departments. The result is to confirm a social stereotype of what the architect is and should be: he or she should be an engineer rather than an artist. This, in turn, throws a fog of ambiguity over the entire idea of expression within architecture. The only acceptable form of expression is one that appears to be scientifically validated: the high-tech style looks exactly like a feat of engineering, even when it employs heroic construction for mundane purposes, as when Nicholas Grimshaw houses a supermarket in Camden under a grand structure suitable for a railroad station. The problem is not helped by the fact that building science has hardly anything of interest to say about the visible form of buildings. For example, energy efficiency is assured primarily by high standards of insulation concealed within the skin, not by a low-energy 'look'. But the British student who wants to justify a 'look' of some kind is forced to exaggerate those technical aspects that can be presented as interesting but not as emanating from a need for self-expression.

The British architect is expected all the same to be full of ideas, to be able to make a contribution; however, the scope of his art is far more limited by his duty to provide competent and well-crafted buildings. In Britain, the door knob that falls off and the roof that leaks are seen as major flaws in the architectural concept. When, as a student at Liverpool University, I showed an appreciation of the ideas of Le Corbusier, as did many of my generation, the faculty had an immediate response: You're wasting your time. Don't you know that all his buildings leak? It is true that Le Corbusier has much to answer for in terms of poor buildings and good imitators, but his ideas became part of the myth of modern architecture and thus an inseparable part of modernity itself. The high-tech school, so successful in Britain today, is undoubtedly based on an extension of the functionalist approach that Le Corbusier so energetically promoted.

The British reaction to an architecture of ideas contains an immediate fear of the high cost of ideas and, even more, a moral reprobation of an art that is practiced for the benefit of a professional career but paid for by the client. This moralism views with uneasiness any kind of building that is not understood as a practical answer to practical problems. As a result, British architects tend to identify very strongly with the ideal of a technically competent architecture, one in which everything that is special about the design can be justified as the result of practical considerations and never attributed to anything as inherently arbitrary as artistic impulse. To avow artistic intentions in architecture is a sure way of arousing suspicion that the architect intends to be liberal with the client's money for his own purposes, whether megalomaniacal or merely personal. Artistic intentions, if they exist, must be dissimulated, or at least played down.

Another way of dissimulating artistic intentions is to present them as the result of following age-old traditions of construction, confirmed by centuries of use and enjoyment. This argument is advanced by the classical revivalists. Buildings should not be egregious statements of new technical possibilities, part of an increasingly dubious and violent future in which civil virtues are in decline, but should be part of a structural continuity that helps bind society together and retain existing values. Buildings and streets make up a system of land use that is so complete and extensive that it cannot be exchanged suddenly for a new system, as was proposed by the modernists after the Second World War. The existing environment consists for the most part of buildings that are nondescript and part of the background, and architects should be prepared to design modestly and allow their buildings to merge into that background, unless there is a social reason for them to stand out. The built environment has evolved and should be protected; like the environment, it should be changed only after careful consideration. This point of view has already made inroads into the utopian vision of a rational society, as the popularity of environmental impact studies confirms. New buildings, then, in cases where they represent important institutions, should be distinguished not by their material construction but by their attention to social propriety. They should work for people.

In a strange way, therefore, British architecture tends to polarize into two opposing camps, both of which rely on a technical argument and reject any idea of a free artistic impulse. This may well be the result of media intervention, as the media tend to ignore a vast quantity of mediocre work that follows some kind of path of least resistance and that architects themselves tend to refer to scornfully as 'pseudo-vernacular'. Effectively there appear to be only two visible positions: on the one hand, the high-tech school advocates technical innovation and the use of new materials and methods that may involve risk and can be seen as progressive. Architecture should be something up-to-date, state-of-the-art, equal to the modern world of lasers and computers. This approach is well-received in Britain, and the high-tech school is replete with knights and beloved of the Establishment. On the other hand, the Prince of Wales has championed the cause of a traditional architecture that works because it follows well-tried and tested ways and avoids unnecessary risk altogether. In both cases, it is the practical argument that is emphasised and personal expression that is played down.

In the United States, on the contrary, no architect can truly rise without promoting an image of personal success. Equally, no architect can gain his client's confidence without giving attention to the bottom line – the end cost that permits a cool assessment of value for one's dollar. American design is therefore

Model and photographs of the Hongkong and Shanghai Banking Corporation headquarters, designed by Sir Norman Foster and Partners, and completed in 1986, shown in the exhibition 'New Architecture: Foster Rogers Stirling', Royal Academy of Arts, London, 1986. *Photo: Andy Weiner*

dominated by a down-to-earth realism. Clients occasionally may want to put up an extraordinary building that will present their business as first in the world, but this building is more likely to do so by being higher that anything else around it than by being technologically advanced. The reality of controlling expense is to build rapidly and reduce labour costs. This in practice means a steel frame, from which everything else is hung. What shows in an American building is not the system of construction but an image of the success of the client. This image may be of any style thought appropriate. Polished granite and plate glass can be alternated to convey Gothic or classical, homely or exotic, as required. Michael Graves's Administration Building for the city of Portland, Oregon (1980), makes a virtue of this by alternating punched and strip windows to outline the profile of a giant keystone, thus making an ironic statement about the very act of constructing architecture. This flexibility is not confined to the postmodern school; it extends to all schools. Richard Meier's whiter-than-white buildings, derived from the twenties style of Le Corbusier, are made in exactly the same way, with an outer skin of enamelled steel panels hung from the constructional frame to assure a self-cleaning, permanently youthful appearance, appropriate to the concept of modernism as Le Corbusier defined it – and indeed better than Le Corbusier could achieve, since he preferred exposed concrete as an expression of the building's reality, and concrete does not tend to stay white. Meier therefore uses modern building science not to pioneer new methods of construction but rather to assure the desired image

more competently. In the United States, no design carries weight unless it conveys an image and makes a statement, within the budget and the building schedule. To spend extra money on pioneering new kinds of construction, or in simply celebrating construction, would seem naive. Norman Foster's building for the Hongkong and Shanghai Banking Corporation (1984), in which the visible form derives directly and extravagantly from the structure, appears to American critics an extremely expensive way of conveying an image of the success of the institution.

So what are we to make of an exhibition from Britain that is presented by the Royal Academy of Arts, a body that is by definition concerned with art as a means of expression? Is the architecture in this show to be taken as in some way restricted to a limited kind of British architecture, accepting only traditional values? Clearly this is not the case: works from a variety of 'schools' are presented, including both the high-tech and the classical revivalist. Indeed, within a period of less than twenty years, the Architecture Room of the Royal Academy's annual Summer Show has been transformed from a cabinet of curiosities into virtually the centrepiece of the exhibition. The advance of architecture has not inhibited the continuing popularity of the Summer Show, but has probably contributed to it. Much of the credit for the improved understanding of architecture within the Academy itself must be given to Hugh Casson, who as President demonstrated that architects could be cultured and perceptive and produce marvellous watercolours. The Academy has now elected another distinguished architect, Philip Dowson, as President. One may also take account of the important work done by architects such as Richard Rogers, in his role as Trustee of the Tate Gallery, or the late James Stirling, who was a close friend of Eduardo Paolozzi. Both became Royal Academicians, as did Colin St John Wilson, the architect of the new British Library and a considerable artist as well as an important patron of modern art. One may refer also to the work of the Royal Society of Arts, a sister institution of the Academy concerned with advancing good design and where architecture has assumed a greater importance in recent years.

But a better understanding of the place of architecture within the arts in Britain is not just the result of personal ties and the influence of a few individuals. It must correspond to a changing view of the place of architecture in public life. There has been an increasing interest among the general public in all issues to do with urban development, often sparked by changes in property values or simply by the loss of familiar places. For many people, there may be a profound distrust, a sense that the environment itself is a rolling beast in which nothing can be counted on to stay put and no haven is safe. Ever since the Prince of Wales began to make an issue of the damage that unconsidered commercial development can do to the environment, citizens have become increasingly aware of the importance of good architecture and have come to realise that the incidence of new development is neither manna from heaven nor an immutable condition (like the climate) but is made up of good and bad examples, which they may judge. Through the process of public inquiries, initiated by city planning boards, new schemes have been put to the test more and more by public opinion, and the public is now eager to pass judgement on the buildings, that surround them.

There is still some way to go, however, before the public is able to make insightful judgements about architecture. How a building works in practice is the product of its material construction and its spatial organisation. Most architects will describe their task as the moulding of space. If this process is to attain the status of high art, it will have to encompass something more than simple practicability, the more so since the efficiency of a plan tends to change with time and with different users. Architects themselves are not certain whether they should address themselves to their immediate audience, to some ideal audience or to posterity. All artists have this problem. The success of a play is judged during its run. Some of the best plays judged as literature have had the shortest runs. There are intangible aspects about buildings that can be left as incidental or explored for their value to the human spirit. The Royal Academy has advanced architecture to such a degree that the quality it reveals is assumed to be something more than structural or social efficiency. That leaves a great deal of room for architecture to be interesting as art.

The architectural work displayed at the Royal Academy's Summer Show generally is of two kinds: models – the equivalent of sculpture – and drawings, paintings, and renderings – the equivalent of pictures. The architect who wants to be included in the show thinks very carefully about this. Mere photographs of buildings do not clearly convey an artistic intent in the context of an exhibition. The architect must rival the touch of the artist by doing something special. A tradition has sprung up to meet this problem: the special rendering whose purpose is not so much the seduction of the client, as is the case with most renderings, but the revelation of artistic purpose. Some of these are elaborate confections that recall the thesis presentations of the old Ecole des Beaux-Arts in Paris. Since the time of John Constable it has been recognised that the spontaneous sketch may also encapsulate an artist's vision. Thus the pictures on the

walls encompass a wide range of forms and a variety of interpretations. Often the aspiration to be viewed as art derives more from the presentation than from the reality of the building depicted. This is a phenomenon that has appeared widely over the last twenty-five years, as architects' presentation drawings, and even working drawings, have been put on the market as the equivalent of works of art. Indeed, once conceptual art arrived, it became possible for a mundane technical depiction of a building to take on some of the quality of an interesting enigma, to mystify the viewer in a stimulating way. The work of architecture students on both sides of the Atlantic is now often focussed on the creation of intriguing enigmas. In contrast, most of the models shown are the same ones that originally dazzled the client. Any imputed artistic purpose is veiled behind the strange custom of portraying a segment of the real world as seen from above; these models fascinate the layperson the way model railroads do. The resulting mélange presented by the exhibition covers many styles of architecture and mediates between the personal and the institutional. Just as the Summer Show itself reveals the state of art appreciation in Britain today, the architecture section is highly representative of the public view of architecture.

It is not surprising, perhaps, that as the scope of visual art widens – as the idea of what an art object is becomes more problematical – the architectural process itself should become of interest to artists. Foremost in exploring this ambiguity is the artist Ben Johnson. His hard-line paintings in acrylic of parts of

Ben Johnson, *Structural Trees, Stansted*, 1990. Acrylic on canvas, 1.52 x 1.52m. Commissioned by Ove Arup & Partners

buildings use the architectural quality of the subject as the stimulus for his own art. The work combines a surreal sense of presence (somewhat like the repetitions of the *nouveau roman* of Alain Robbe-Grillet) with a luminous beauty. Johnson's study *Structural Trees* (exhibited in the 1991 Summer Show) is a beautiful object in its own right, but it also celebrates the elegance of Norman Foster's design for Stansted Airport (exhibited in 1990). The result is quite different from an architect's perspectival rendering; it does not work to sell the design but rather to reveal its quality. Similarly, Brendan Neiland, in his silk-screen print *Cumulus* (exhibited in 1991), recreates the view upward to the sky, seen through a glazed roof, as a mysterious experience. Closely related to this work, as an object of contemplation, is Jonathan Gray's computer-generated perspectival rendering of the proposed Ashford International Passenger Station for the Channel Tunnel (exhibited in 1991). The experience it projects is not of a simple reality, but of a kind of hyper-reality that is surreal in its implications. The convergence of the artist's view of the building and the architect's vision of the project defines an ambiguous experience – part art, part dream.

Colin St John Wilson, The British Library, St Pancras: Panoramic Painting, 1991. Mixed media

Robert Adam, Solar House at Wakeham, West Sussex, 1993. Ink drawing

The artist's interest in architecture is balanced by the architect's interest in art. Colin St John Wilson, an architect, has produced a number of imaginative pictures that explore the steps of the design process. His *Tyranny of Perspective* (exhibited in 1992) demonstrates the unyielding rules of visual perception, which encompass the expression of the architect rather than that of the visual artist. However it also does so in a way that questions these rules and creates an interesting space, a kind of psychological thriller. A similar effect is produced in his model of *The King's Library* (exhibited in 1993), in which a red lay figure enacts the ergonomic rituals of shelf access. His painting *Panoramic of the British Library* (exhibited in 1991) integrates impressions of the building with a Piranesian sense of merging spaces. In all these cases the work of the architect appears not as a professional quest for fees but as an intellectual quest for the trappings of reality, which, once thought to be so obvious, are now to be seen as mysterious as language itself.

Strict modernist architects such as Colin St John Wilson tend to reveal the mysteries in the process. The classicists tend to assert its social status period. Robert Adam's presentation drawing, *Solar House at Wakeham, West Sussex* (exhibited in 1993), includes portraits of the architect and his assistants gravely bearing plans and elevations, making a solemn visit to the completed building; a Corinthian capital lies in the grass at their feet. Thus the multiple drawing beloved by the Beaux-Arts is recreated as a mundane experience, the experience of a site visit. Even here, however, one finds a redeeming irony. The drawings borne by the personages are less real than the perspective of the completed house, and we are again asked to contemplate a linguistic ambiguity along with the process of building, which is, after all, a practical routine for materialising the future. There is also a little joke, for the solar house is usually presented as a scientific achievement, not as the result of building a neoclassical or mannerist villa. Another example of this kind of ironic framing, which allows

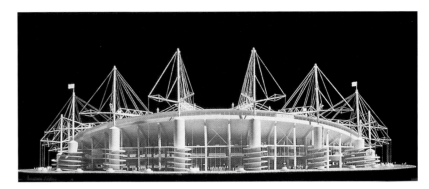

Model of Arup Associates's project for the Manchester Olympic 2000 Amec Stadium, 1992

a partial resurrection of the symbolic, is the *Continuing Study for the House at Rotherhithe* by Timpson, Manley, Deans (exhibited in 1991). Here, the elevation of the building is shut up in a box together with damaged building components, part of a chain, and rusted steel fragments, inducing a sense of *memento mori* in a presentation in which the new quickly becomes the old. The conceit allows the building, prosaic in its ordinary implications, to be rendered in a more poetic vein.

The perceived leader of the classical revivalists is the architect Quinlan Terry. However, while he is eager to insist on the continuity of architecture as a language, he is not averse to asserting the peculiar opportunities of the modern age as an instigation for the outsize venture. His project for the new Brentwood Cathedral is as extravagant as his grasp of the classical is flexible. More characteristic of the Academy's taste is the modesty of expression found in Ian Barker's drawing for the Leonard Manasseh Partnership, *Cantilevered Footbridge: New Research Centre for British*

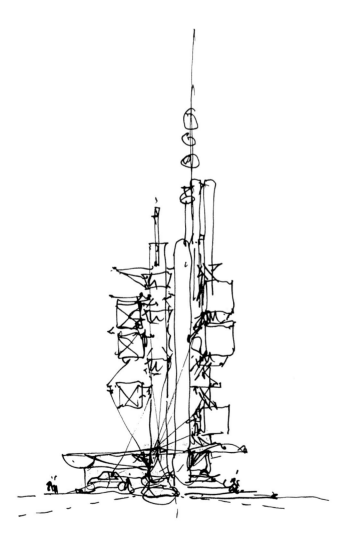

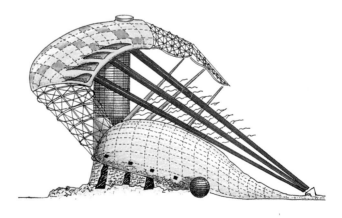

Birds Portchmouth Russum Architects's shrimp-like 'Theatre' for their Morecambe Seafront project, 1991. Crayon and ink drawing

Richard Rogers Partnership, K-1 Tower Exhibition Space, Tomigaya, Tokyo, 1990. Sketch of the building by Laurie Abbott

Model of the Marylebone Gate scheme by Michael Hopkins and Partners, commissioned in 1989. Model: Tetra

Gas, Loughborough, in which the building portrayed is glimpsed, almost incidentally, as part of the idyllic experience of a spring day.

On the whole, though, the Academy's choices express a preference for architecture that comes directly out of the structural system, and in this it conforms to some extent with a characterisation of the British scene as one not a little inhibited by the idea of architecture as art. No one can be other than impressed by Arup Associates's project for the Manchester Olympic 2000 Amec Stadium (exhibited in 1993). This is a triumph of engineering, but also of architecture, through the boldness of the forms: The shell of the seating and the rhythm of the access ramps contribute as much as the structural ingenuity of the pylons. No one feels embarrassed by the thought that this enormous structure has been rendered into poetry, only grateful. On the other hand, in Richard Rogers's K1 Tower Exhibition Space in Tomigaya, Tokyo (exhibited in 1991), the heroic structure is not required by the programme but advanced by the architect as a value. The result, by some alchemy, is quintessentially Japanese. It also uses the structural form to produce the kind of equivocal clash of elements that brings the design close to the camp of the deconstructivists. The same tendency is visible in the Morecambe Seafront project by Birds Portchmouth Russum Architects (exhibited in 1993), in which the structural form is less rational and more overtly expressionist in character. It is no surprise to find that expressionism, too, appears in Britain under a structural banner.

There is also some development of a more moderate view of architecture as a social amenity, accomplished not by adopting traditional forms but by applying modern rationalism with a sense of context.

Of the high-tech school, Michael Hopkins is a good example of this trend. His practice's building for the Lords Cricket Club in London is celebrated for creating a wonderful succession of different characters, encountered as the eye travels up the face of the building, recalling Alberti's didactic presentation of the superimposed orders of architecture in the Palazzo Rucellai. The architects' scheme for Marylebone Gate (exhibited in 1992) is modern in feeling, but resuscitates the classical arrangement of a rotunda within a square block. The design allows us to envisage the continuation of modernity without sacrificing continuity with the past. A team combining a similar sense of the history of architecture with an acutely modern sense of the social opportunities of today is that of Jeremy Dixon and Edward Jones. The photograph of the maquette of their scheme for a bus station, Piazzale Roma, Venice (exhibited in 1992), conveys a perfect blend of efficiency and discretion.

Perhaps the most encouraging evidence of the change of climate that is beginning to allow architecture to be seen as an art is the induction into the Academy of the late James Stirling. His frank avowal of artistic intention tended to make him a figure of suspicion on the English scene. Stirling, more than anyone else, however, stated a position that allows continuity with the past to coexist with a sharp sense of the efficient use of space. His little Electa Bookshop in the Biennale Gardens, Venice (exhibited in 1993), is a miracle of succinctness, both as a facility for use

Jeremy Dixon . Edward Jones, Bus station at the Piazzale Roma, Venice, 1991. Drawing in crayon on brown paper by David Naessens

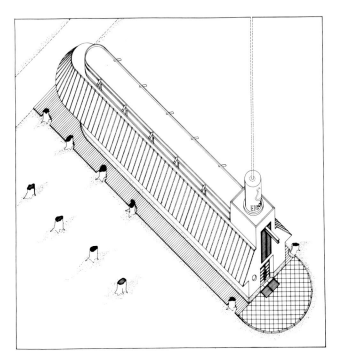

James Stirling Michael Wilford and Associates, Bookshop for the Venice Biennale, 1992. Axonometric drawing

and as an evocation of architecture. It promotes an architecture that is simultaneously art and amenity.

Does the Academy's Summer Show tell us anything about the future development of architecture in Britain? What styles are on the way out, what architects are on the way in? No, only by the interposition of a personal viewpoint. Today the great question in architecture within the developed countries relates to the question of renewal. Is it the case, as the traditionalists maintain, that the investment in ordinary buildings is so overwhelming and the preservation of the continuity of the environment so important that we must reject the unique building that aggressively projects its own innate complexity and hangs the consequences? At the height of the modern movement there was no doubt in architects' minds that they were building the future, and that the future would be different from today, and bigger. One thinks of the linear city of the American architect Paul Rudolph, which took the form of a single, enormous building with a characteristic cross-section that eventually would extend the entire length of the northeast corri-

dor from Washington D.C., to Boston. That was typical of the expanding view of architecture prevalent during the 1960s. The change in architectural expression, visible both in Britain and in the United States, is away from entire environments and towards the individual building. The emphasis is less on outward connections, more on inward qualities. In cases in which the building is isolated, as with Foster's Stansted Airport, outside London, the form is generated from the internal process and creates no problem for the surrounding environment. Where the building is part of a dense city, as with Rogers's headquarters for Lloyd's in the City of London, the question of 'fitting in' or 'standing out' becomes crucial. There does seem to be a future for buildings that, whether they stand out or fit in, create a better appreciation of the quality of space and of the varieties of spatial experience. The question of style may therefore be less important in the future than the question of quality.

Local newspapers are full nowadays of stories on environmental issues, and public interest in new building is growing along with an increasing awareness of the way buildings can spoil and improve the quality of life. The Royal Academy, however, is not promoting architecture purely out of a sense of social responsibility, with the aim of improving the local scene. Its mission is to promote the arts, and this mission is entwined with the mission of art, if we can speak in those terms. Art is concerned with the highest aspirations, and, in a secular age, it assumes much of the responsibility for spiritual regeneration. Architecture, as long as it remains a mere utility or an aspect of real estate transactions, cannot easily be admitted to this realm. But there is no reason why, while attending to realities, it cannot also aspire to other things. During the Renaissance, artists and architects spoke with the same voice. By its emphasis on the materiality of building, the modern movement reduced architecture to a branch of technology. Today, when the status of the art object is no longer unquestioned, it is possible to view buildings as another channel of expression and as prime evidence for the future anthropologist who seeks to come to terms with the culture of the twenty-first century. The Royal Academy provides a framework in which architecture can be judged on the highest terms.

Projects

Robert Adam's
presentation drawing

Manor Farm is a typical English manor house. The original building dates from the fifteenth century. While many medieval features remain, the house has been extended and altered regularly in its six-hundred-year history. This latest addition provides a large drawing room, a master bedroom, and various improved facilities.

The main entrance to Manor Farm is through its west side via the original farmyard. The east side faces rolling pastures, typical of southern England. The oldest parts of the house are on the west side, and it was decided that the new extensions should look out over the countryside, minimising the impact on the old building. At the same time, it was felt that the casual extension of the old house could not be continued without losing the significance of the older parts and that the extensions should complement and contrast with the existing building.

A large number of alternative plans and elevations were investigated. The final scheme has a strong, individual character, quite different from the existing building, while employing the same materials used as part of its structure in a classical manner.

The west elevation

Extension to Manor Farm, Weston Patrick, Hampshire

Robert Adam

Building commenced 1993
Commissioned 1991
Completed 1994
Client Sir Thomas and Lady Stockdale
Main Contractor Thos. King & Sons (Builders) Ltd

View of the west frontage of Manor Farm

Ian Sutherland's drawing
of the completed bridge

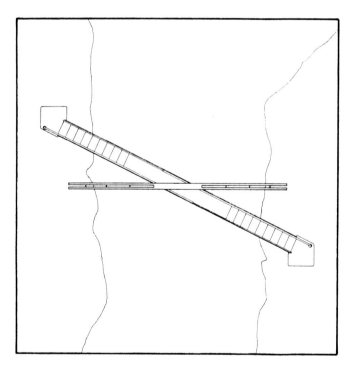

Plan

Thames Path Footbridge, London

Allies and Morrison Architects

Competition 1993
Client The Countryside Commission
Engineer Atelier One
Quantity Surveyor Gavin Charlesworth, Boyden & Co.

Allies and Morrison's competition design for a new
public footbridge over the River Thames in the open
countryside near Oxford is composed of two discrete
parts: a structural arch that supports the centre of the
bridge, and a pedestrian deck that passes beneath the
arch. In plan, the arch and the deck are placed at an
angle to one another. The arch spans orthogonally
from bank to bank, while the deck crosses the river
at an angle. The diagonal route of the deck thereby
engages naturally with the flow of the footpath on
either side of the river; in contrast, the structural arch
spans the river in a straightforward manner.
The pedestrian deck is constructed from unfinished
heartwood oak sections that have been pin-jointed
to form a complex vierendeel structure. The arch is
formed by a pair of composite beams with shear
sections made of glue-laminated timber and flanges
made of stainless steel plate. From a fixing between
the beams, two stainless steel hangers support the
deck at the centre of its span, cradling the timber
lattice as it passes under the arch and reducing its
bending moment by a factor of four.

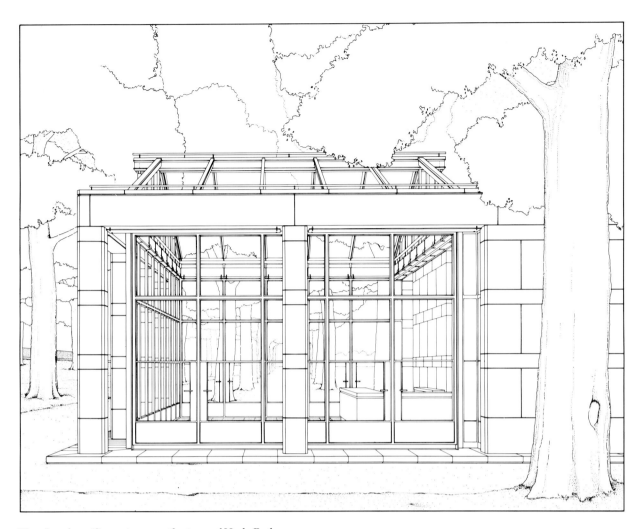

The glazed pavilion set among the trees of Hyde Park

Pavilion in Hyde Park, London

Allies and Morrison Architects

Competition 1989
Client *The Central Electricity Generating Board*
Quantity Surveyor *E. C. Harris & Partners*

Allies and Morrison was one of three architectural practices selected to prepare designs for ventilation shaft headwork for a new cross-London electricity cable tunnel. The two structures stand like pavilions in the landscape in the manner of eighteenth-century English garden buildings. Each relates to its surroundings by becoming a focus for activities: The pavilion accommodates a small café at the edge of the green spaces of the park, framed by a canopy of surrounding trees. While the ventilation shaft to the right of the perspective, along with the columns, are faced in Portland stone, the café is predominantly glazed and is seen as a free-standing structure set within the enclosing colonnade. In the summer the café opens out onto the pedestrian thoroughfare of the Broad Walk.

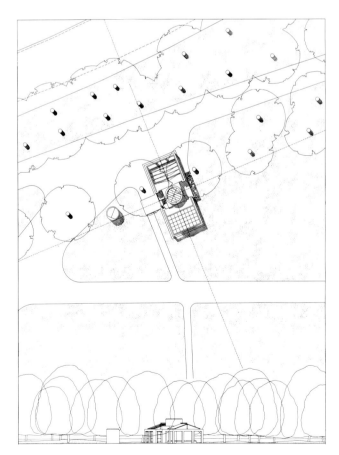

Plan

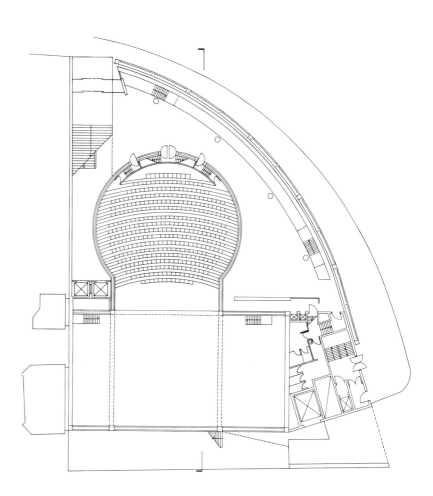

Second floor plan, showing exhibition hall

Ground floor plan, showing theatre and
seminar hall and adjoining restaurant

Maison de la Culture du Japon, Paris
Armstrong Architects

Competition 1990
Building commenced 1994
Completion due 1996
Client Association pour la Construction de la Maison
de la Culture du Japon à Paris

The competition for the Maison de la Culture
du Japon was initiated by President François
Mitterand of France with Zenko Suzuki, the
Prime Minister of Japan, in 1982. A brief was
devised, and an open international competition
was launched in September 1989 for the design
of a cultural centre for Japan on one of the last
remaining sites next to the Seine in the middle
of Paris. The winning design by Armstrong
Architects includes a 450-seat theatre, an exhibition space, a library and médiathèque,
seminar rooms, an office, a shop, and a restaurant. The total net area is to be 7,500 square
metres on a quadrant-shaped footprint of 1,670
square metres. The building is the last of the
Parisian Grands Projets and is planned for
completion in 1996.

Isometric drawing

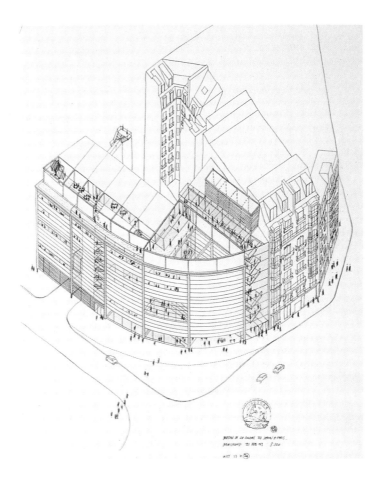

Model of the Maison de la Culture du Japon,
superimposed on a photograph, showing the
building in its Parisian context

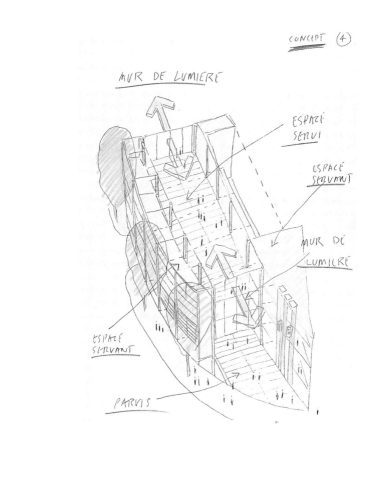

CONCEPT (4)

MUR DE LUMIERE

ESPACE SERVI

ESPACE SERVANT

MUR DE LUMIERE

ESPACE SERVANT

PARVIS

Diagrammatic sketch of the building,
showing the exhibition level

opposite:
Model of building and site, from the east,
looking onto sports ground to the left

Longitudinal section through the building,
showing theatre and seminar hall

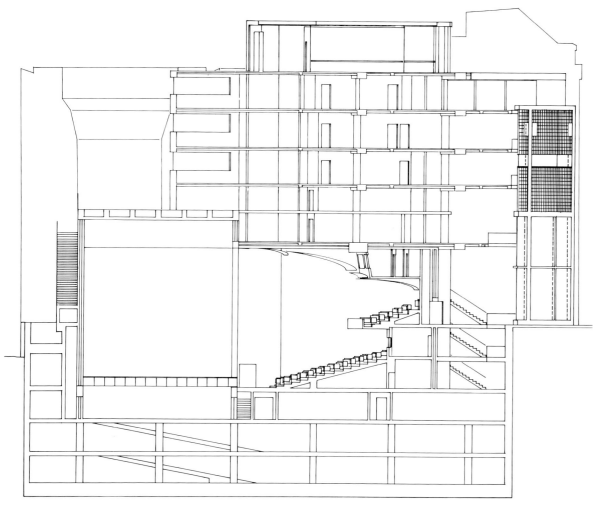

Computer-generated image of the
Symphony Hall, which seats 2,500

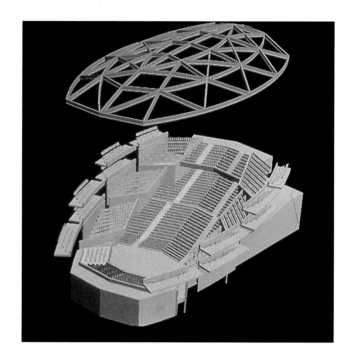

Bird's-eye view of the model of the Symphony Hall

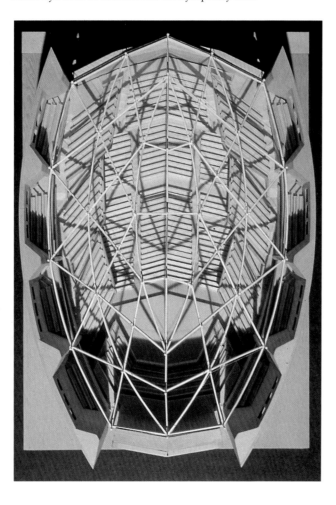

Istanbul Kültür Merkezi

Arup Associates

Competition 1990
Building to commence 1994
Client The Istanbul Foundation for Culture and Arts
Engineers and Quantity Surveyors Arup Associates
Acoustic Consultants Arup Acoustics

Arup Associates developed their proposal for an invited
international competition in 1990. The Istanbul Kültür
Merkezi, the new Cultural Centre for the Istanbul Foundation for Culture and Arts at Ayazaga Kasri will create
a national landmark for Turkey and enhance its rich
cultural heritage. The design includes a symphony hall
for 2,500; two smaller conference halls, to seat 500 and
300; a hall for chamber music seating 450; and a small
cinema. The centre is on a beautiful woodland site, formerly the Sultan's retreat, located on the outskirts of
the city; it will incorporate two existing historic houses.
The Cavalry House and the Ayazaga Mansion will be
restored to accommodate amenities and offices for the
Foundation. The Çinili Kösk, an elegant timber pavilion,
and an adjacent pleasure pool at the heart of the site will
also be restored. Together with a series of terraced gardens and an outdoor amphitheatre, these will serve as a
focus for the scheme.

Legal & General House, Kingswood, Surrey

Arup Associates

Commissioned 1985
Building commenced 1986
Completed 1991
Client *Legal & General Assurance Society Ltd*
Engineers and Quantity Surveyors *Arup Associates*
Main Contractor *Taylor Woodrow Management Ltd*
Landscape Consultant *Peter Swann & Associates*

The rotunda roof

Model of the rotunda entrance

Legal & General House is the new headquarters for the Legal & General Assurance Society, providing office space for a staff of 1,500. The brief for the building called for 24,000 square metres of space on three levels surrounding two landscaped courtyards. The uppermost floors house the offices and 8,000 square metres of ancillary support space — including computer rooms, storage and restaurant facilities — are located on the lower floor. The project included the restoration of a large Edwardian house next to the headquarters, to create a residential staff-training centre. In addition, a number of recreational facilities for employees have been designed, with landscaped sports fields, tennis courts, pavilion housing areas for changing and eating, a swimming pool, and a sports hall. The building was designed with particular attention to energy efficiency. External sunscreens reduce solar gain, and the heat storage system uses the staff swimming pool as a heat sink.

View from the open countryside. *Photo: Peter Cook*

The stadium, with a one-kilometre circumference and seating for 80,000 spectators, was proposed as a focal building in Manchester's unsuccessful bid to host the 2000 Olympics. A circular seating plan combines with an oval arena to create elevations that sweep up from the north and south to contain four key levels to the east and west. The high sides of the stadium provide protection from the prevailing winds and low sun angles, while concentrating seating and amenities in the areas most favoured by spectators. The low sides allow light onto the grassed arena for photosynthesis and give a human scale to the structure. The shape of the building creates a landmark on the flat site, offering a point of focus for spectators approaching from the new public transport system.

The scheme includes a landscaped circulation space surrounding the entire stadium. From this area people arriving to view events can be directed into zones defined by large round towers wrapped by open circulation ramps that afford startling views across the Olympic City. The towers combine circulation with a mast-and-cable roof structure to create a visual order and enhance crowd comfort and safety. They provide the stadium with an image that both by day and night — when spectacularly lit — is intended to highlight the Olympic idyll.

Model of the stadium

Manchester 2000 Olympic Stadium

Arup Associates

Commissioned 1992
Stadium design Arup Associates, in association with HOK Sports Facilities Group
Developer AMEC Developments plc

Computer-generated image by Hayes-Davidson of the stadium as seen by night

Sussex Grandstand, Goodwood Racecourse, Sussex

Arup Associates

Commissioned 1988
Building commenced 1989
Completed 1990
Client Goodwood Racecourse Ltd
Engineers and Quantity Surveyors Arup Associates
Specialist Steelwork Fabricator
    Littlehampton Welding Ltd.
Fabric Structures KOIT
General Contractor James Longley Ltd

View of stand from the racecourse
Photo: Peter Cook

In 1988 Arup Associates was appointed to prepare a master plan for Goodwood Racecourse. As part of the second phase of the plan, a new stand with a high viewing position was designed, and also a members' restaurant that would command a good seated view of the course. All enclosures were to be extended and improved. The canopy gives the stand its main character. This permanent translucent tent is intended to become the largest of the canopies that appear each season, around which the many other marquees will be clustered. Soft in silhouette, it is light in structure. The clear glass windshields surrounding the high-level seating and the canopied area give a feeling of openness conducive to a festive atmosphere. Together with white-painted steelwork, the building provides a bright and airy spot in which to enjoy the races and the magnificent landscape. The lower steppings give direct access to the lawns, the paddock, and the bookmakers' forecourt as well as to the comprehensive support facilities on the ground floor.

The canopy is the stand's identifying feature. *Photo: Sir Philip Dowson*

Stonehenge Visitors' Centre

Birds Portchmouth Russum Architects

Competition 1992
Client English Heritage
Structural Engineer Matthew Wells
Services Engineer Ove Arup and Partners
Traffic Engineers Ove Arup and Partners
Landscape Consultants John Duane Architects

The design of the visitors' centre is inspired by the archaeological context of the 'henge' monuments prehistoric manmade enclosures set in clearings in a woodland forest. The visitors' centre is conceived as a contemporary settlement within a forest offering shelter from the exposed conditions of Salisbury Plain and from which visitors make the transition from the world of the automobile into the primeval landscape. The centre itself forms a clearing, oval in shape and sunk into the hill on one side, while emerging as a protective wall to com-

plete the enclosure on the other. This clearing is articulated by a colonnade and is located at a low point on the site to ensure that the visitors' centre is concealed from the monument of Stonehenge. The centre is oriented at a ninety-degree angle to Stonehenge Avenue to reduce exposure to the prevailing winds.

The car park and access road are set beneath an umbrella of new woodland plantings, introduced progressively to replace the existing regiment of conifers. The car park is subdivided into small glades that connect with a path winding through the woodland to the visitors' centre. The path slopes down into a cutting that leads into the circular entrance loggia. Here, one can move around the ambulatory colonnade following a sequential route or cross the open courtyard to the exit which leads to the monument. The entrance loggia provides visitors with direct access to the orientation and information areas, the lecture theatre, the camera obscura, and the educational facilities before departure to Stonehenge. Visitors returning from the monument proceed through a colonnade to the exhibition area, restaurant, and shops.

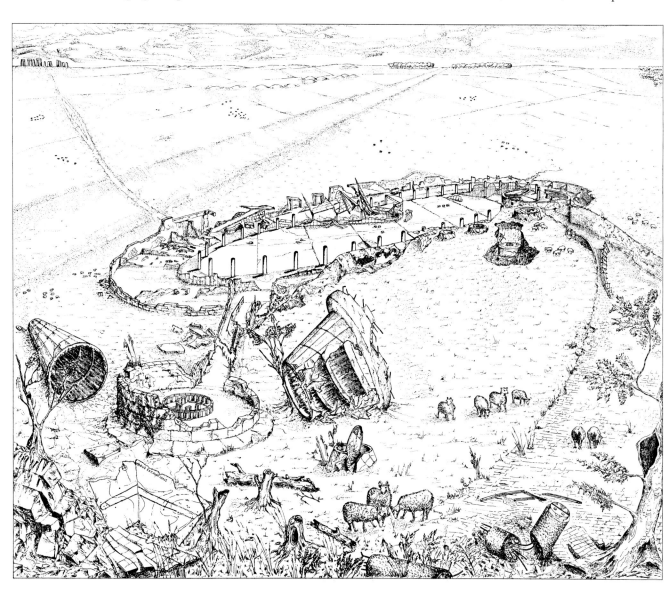

Archaeological landscape: ink drawing of the Centre as it might be in several thousand years' time

Ink drawing of the camera obscura

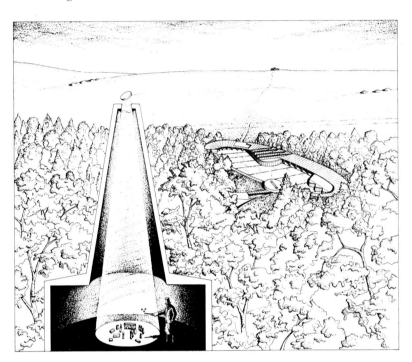

Axonometric drawing looking south.
The centre is sunk into the side of the hill.
above and below: drawings in crayon and ink

A colonnade lines
the interior of the oval

A series of 'shrimp' buildings line the
promenade, including this amusement hall.
above and below: drawings rendered in crayon and ink

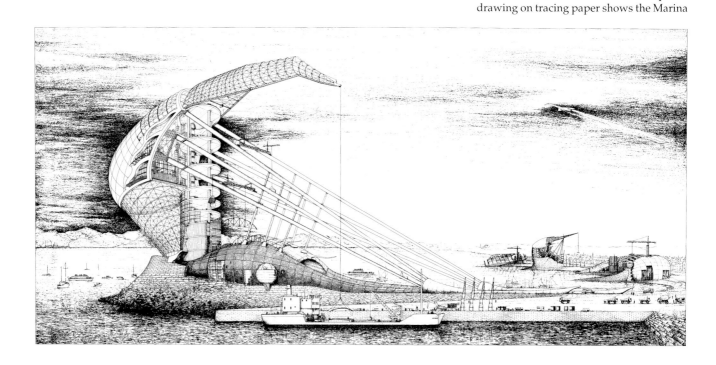

A life-boat station. The 'shrimp' buildings can
be constructed in a phased development

The dramatic 'shrimp' structures are designed to
stimulate the revival of Morecambe. This pencil
drawing on tracing paper shows the Marina

Morecambe Seafront

Birds Portchmouth Russum Architects

Competition 1991
Client Lancaster City Council
Traffic Engineer Ove Arup and Partners
Landscape Architect David Samuel

Morecambe is a popular seaside resort in the north east of England. Reconstruction of the seafront to protect the town against coastal erosion will result in significant visual change to Morecambe Bay and introduces the opportunity to look at proposals intended to stimulate a revival of the resort.

For a competition held in 1991 to generate ideas, Birds Portchmouth Russum proposed large, fantastic 'shrimp-like' constructions to be located on the breakwater, silhouetted against the backdrop of the Lake District, the Bay, and the town itself. Each symbolises one of the four original villages that merged to form Morecambe. These constructions present a dynamic and cohesive foreground and are designed to accommodate new marina facilities, an amusement arcade, a multipurpose theatre and concert hall, and a fireboat station.

A newly created promenade runs along the shoreline, linking the 'shrimp' buildings. Consisting of a tree-lined boardwalk, the pier (replacing the existing central pier, which is no longer viable) offers a stage setting for promenaders, seafood stalls, and ice cream vendors. The proposal provides a simple and spectacular strategic concept for the development of Morecambe's seafront. The boardwalk promenade and surrounding landscaping does not require expensive technological solutions. The shrimp buildings can be constructed easily in a phased development and are suitable for private investment.

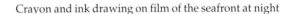

Crayon and ink drawing on film of the seafront at night

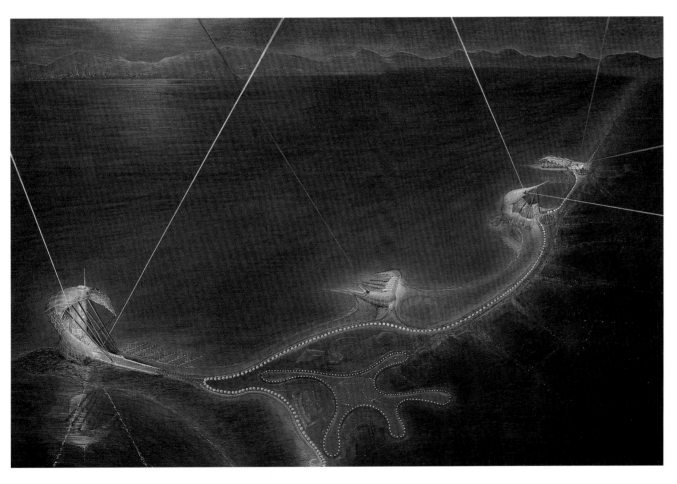

All England Lawn Tennis and Croquet Club, Masterplan, Wimbledon

Building Design Partnership (BDP)

Commissioned 1992
Phase one to commence 1994
Client *The All England Lawn Tennis and Croquet Club, Wimbledon*
Structural and Services Engineers *Building Design Partnership*
Quantity Surveyor *Monk Dunstone Associates*
Landscape Architects *Building Design Partnership*

To ensure that Wimbledon maintains its leadership as the premier tennis tournament, the All England Club commissioned Building Design Partnership to design a masterplan for Wimbledon Church Road and to improve the quality of the event for players, spectators, media, officials, and neighbours. The brief was to create a more relaxed, quintessentially Wimbledon character, described as 'tennis in an English garden'. There was also the need to carve out clear patterns of movement and generous space to provide comfort and safety for all. The architects planned the grounds as 'a country house in its garden', with Centre Court, the actual and symbolic heart, being strengthened visually by serving as the big house. All other elements function as outbuildings

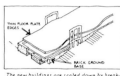 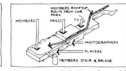

The new buildings are scaled down by break-ing them into horizontal layers *Many groups use the building: players, club members, press, photographers, television* *Entrances and cores are marked mental topiary elements*

FACILITIES BUILDING

Aerial view of the All England Lawn Tennis and Croquet Club grounds at Wimbledon

Centre Court, the actual and symbolic heart – *is to be strengthened visually to be the 'big house'* *Segregated links to the new Facilities Build*

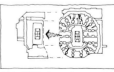 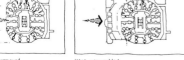 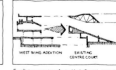

Existing No.1 Court removed *West wing added* *Facilities previously in No.1 Court are ad plus seating*

CENTRE COURT EXTENSION

or garden structures and defer to the main 'house'. The spaces between the buildings, the outer courts, act as the formal gardens.

The basic organisation sets Centre Court within a ladder pattern of major pathways. This allows the spectators to be spread more evenly over the grounds, giving space in which to move about and providing clear orientation. The masterplan suggests a theatre-like differentiation between 'front and back of house'. Public access is focussed on the east and the service circulation and main facilities on the west, partly below rising ground to give the illusion of a continuous garden.

A new facilities building accommodates players, club members, and the media, who access other buildings by bridges or underpasses, thereby reducing congestion considerably at ground level for the public. The structure extends northwards under the rising ground, cutting into the hillside. Internally, the service cores, plant, kitchens, and underground service routes are located on the west side of the building.

Centre Court is to be extended to the west with additional seating, relocating and enhancing facilities previously contained within the No. 1 Court. Circulation routes within Centre Court are complex, and its access to the new No. 1 Court and facilities building have been rationalised, enabling segregated passage for players, officials, and important guests.

re-emphasises the back of house/ concept of the masterplan

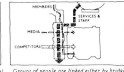
Groups of people are linked either by bridges or underground routes to other buildings

The building cuts into the hillside maintaining views across the site

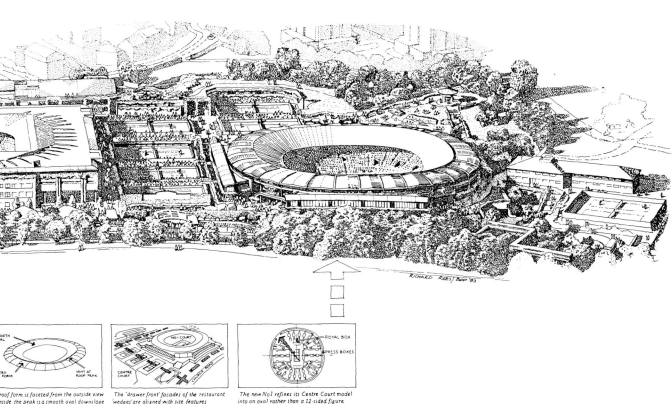

RICHARD ROGERS PARTNERSHIP '93

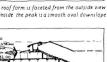
roof form is faceted from the outside view inside the peak is a smooth oval downslope

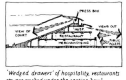
The 'drawer front' facades of the restaurant 'wedges' are aligned with site features

The new No1 refines its Centre Court model into an oval rather than a 12-sided figure.

new court is countersunk into the hillside

'Wedged drawers' of hospitality, restaurants etc are pushed under the seating bowl

Circulation is rationalised

EW NO.1. COURT

Headquarters for Adam Opel AG, Rüsselsheim, Germany

Building Design Partnership (BDP)

Commissioned 1993
Collaborating Architects Planungsbüro Rohling, Nägle Hofmann
　　　　　　Tiedermann und Partner
Client Adam Opel AG
Structural and Services Engineers Building Design Partnership
Quantity Surveyors Building Design Partnership

The 38,000-square-metre building replaces Adam Opel's offices in its old plant, which are to be redeveloped commercially. The new headquarters will form part of a complex composed of existing and new company buildings arranged around a central green space. Building Design Partnership was selected for the project as the result of an ideas competition held among eight international architectural practices. The key features in the winning design are its large floor plate; a low-rise pattern for ease of communications and a democratic work style; a central 'heart' space for displays, a reception area, and team interaction; good commercial asset value; and a sensitivity to the architecture of the town. The architects are also working on the design of an amenities pavilion, which will include a staff restaurant and an Opel museum, and on general improvements to the complex.

above, right, and opposite:
preliminary visuals by Gareth Jones in the form of mixed media collages with crayon on paper of the museum and amenities pavilion at Adam Opel AG's headquarters complex

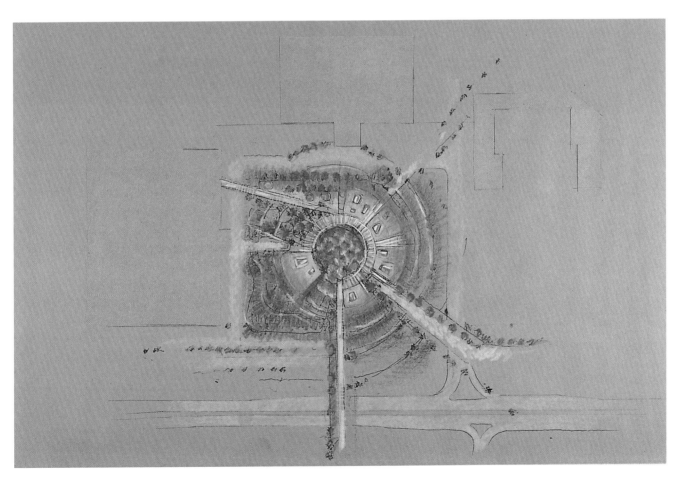

Refurbishment of the Foreign and Commonwealth Office, London

Conservation Architects: Cecil Denny Highton

Commissioned 1980
Commenced 1980
Completion due 1996
Client *Foreign and Commonwealth Office*

The renovation of the Foreign and Commonwealth Office is one of the most extensive projects of its kind undertaken in recent years. Formerly known as the Old Public Offices, the building was originally home to the India Office, the Foreign Office, the Home Office, and the Colonial Office. Designed by Sir George Gilbert Scott, the ministerial departments were built between 1862 and 1874 as four separate sets of offices around a large central carriage court. The entire building is now occupied by the Foreign Office.

The renovation has restored Scott's masterpiece to its former glory while carefully integrating the paraphernalia of a contemporary office building. Scott's use of lavish decorations to impress foreign visitors is exemplified in the Grand Staircase, or Ambassador's Stair. it is used by new ambassadors bringing their letters of introduction to the Foreign Secretary. The stair also leads to other ministerial rooms and a magnificent set of reception rooms.

The main area, three storeys high, is a combination of marble, chrome-red paint, and gold leaf surmounted by a vast dome decorated with female figures representing the countries that had diplomatic relations with Great Britain in the 1860s. The Oval Room was originally designed as the office for the Secretary of State of India; the interior is by Sir Matthew Digby Wyatt, the Surveyor of the East India Company. The gold leaf used on the domed ceiling and on decorations elsewhere in the room reflected the wealth of visitors from the Indian subcontinent during the latter half of the nineteenth century. An unusual feature of the room is a pair of doors, said to have been installed so that two visiting princes of equal rank could be received simultaneously with neither losing precedence.

The recently restored grand staircase
Photo: Adam Woolfit

The Oval Room designed by Sir Matthew Digby Wyatt
Photo: Adam Woolfit

Five Centuries of Drapers' Hall, City of London

Robert Chitham, Chapman Taylor Partners

Drawn research project 1993
Client *The Worshipful Company of Drapers*

The Drapers' Company has occupied the same site in Throgmorton Street in the City of London since 1543. The research project stemmed from a suggestion that models be made showing the form of Drapers' Hall in all its manifestations since that date, the premises having undergone major rebuilding on four occasions. Although the company's archives are unusually comprehensive, there was insufficient evidence to provide the basis for an authentic series of models. In particular, no detailed plans exist of the hall as it was rebuilt after the Great Fire of London in 1666, or as it was again rebuilt after a major fire in 1772.

A reasonable representation could be made, however, of the street elevation at each phase of the hall's existence, although in the case of the first hall this was to some extent necessarily conjectural. A detailed and dimensioned ground-floor plan from 1630 survives, as does an earlier written description. These, together with information on contemporary palaces and houses, and pictorial representations provided by early maps of the City of London, permitted the outlines of the building to be drawn, although not in detail.

Documentation of the building after the Great Fire of London relies largely on drawings prepared by the architect John Gorham showing how the old building could be restored. Ultimately restoration was abandoned in favour of rebuilding. The eighteenth-century facade, in turn, is well illustrated by measured drawings of perspectives found in the company's archives. Good photographic records also exist, as well as some contract drawings of the short-lived building of the mid-nineteenth century.

Pen and watercolour drawings by Robert Chitham
of the Drapers' Hall through the ages 1543-1993

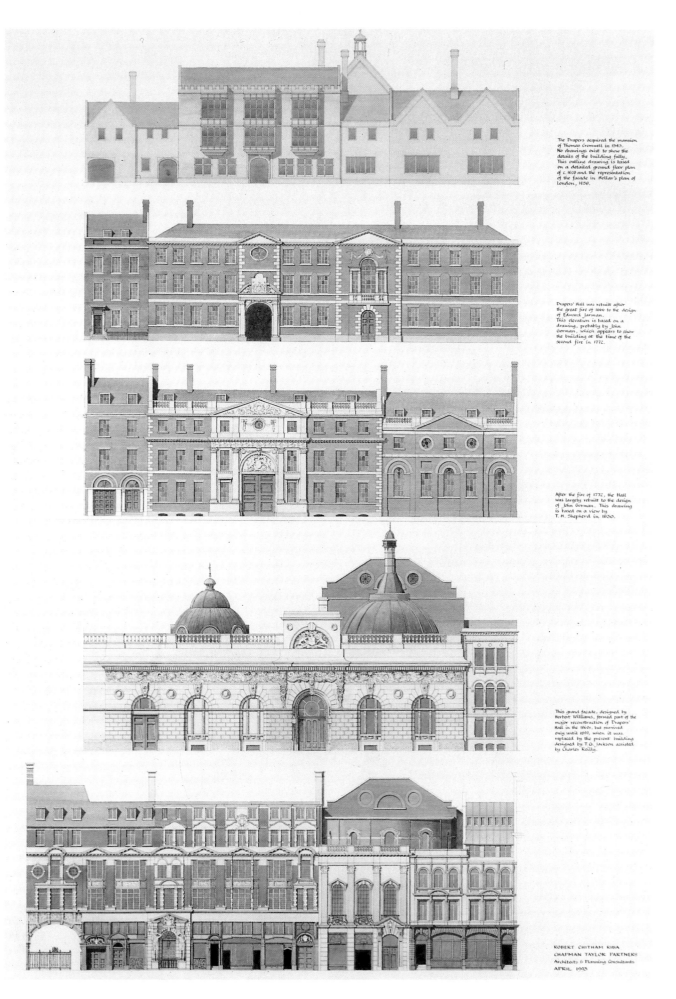

The Drapers acquired the mansion of Thomas Cromwell in 1543. No drawings exist to show the details of the building fully. This outline drawing is based on a detailed ground floor plan of c.1600 and the representation of the façade in Hollar's plan of London, 1658.

Drapers' Hall was rebuilt after the great fire of 1666 to the design of Edward Jarman. This elevation is based on a drawing, probably by John Gorman, which appears to show the building at the time of the second fire in 1772.

After the fire of 1772, the Hall was largely rebuilt to the design of John Gorman. This drawing is based on a view by T. H. Shepherd in 1830.

This grand façade, designed by Herbert Williams, formed part of the major reconstruction of Drapers' Hall in the 1860s, but survived only until 1897, when it was replaced by the present building designed by T. G. Jackson assisted by Charles Reilly.

ROBERT CHITHAM RIBA
CHAPMAN TAYLOR PARTNERS
Architects & Planning Consultants
APRIL 1995

Flat Conversion, London
Simon Conder Associates

Commissioned 1992
Completion 1993
Main Contractor Coniston Ltd
Structural Engineer Malcolm Millais

The client wanted to create a private area at the top of her nineteenth-century ter-raced house in Primrose Hill that would take full advantage of the previously unused roof space and the fine views to the rear. The design creates a large multipurpose space on two levels. The original roof structure and the internal walls on the third level have been re-moved and replaced by a new steel-framed roof structure incorporating a large skylight. A steel-framed sleeping gallery with a new storage wall along-side the party wall — holding ward-robes, bookshelves, and a freestanding oval glass bathroom — were introduced into the space. The bathroom provides a degree of separation between the study area at the rear and the larger living space at the front of the plan; at night it provides the primary light sources for the space as a whole.

The bathroom interior
Photo: Jo Reid and John Peck

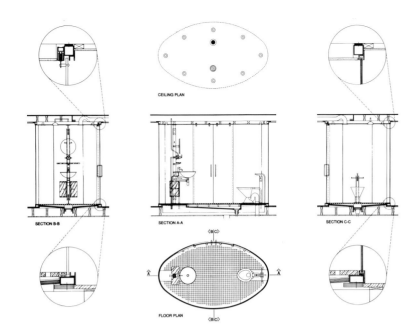

CEILING PLAN

SECTION B-B   SECTION A-A   SECTION C-C

FLOOR PLAN

Plans, section and details

Axonometric

At night the bathroom
provides the primary light source
Photo: Jo Reid and John Peck

Breitscheidplatz, Berlin

Peter Cook

Commission for magazine 1990

This project was the result of a commission from the German magazine *Geo*. The magazine asked a number of designers to look at a public space in Berlin and propose ideas for environmental improvements. Cook selected the Breitscheidplatz, a familiar landmark that surrounds the ruins of the Kaiserkapelle and its additions by Egon Eiermann. It is a busy place but characterless, with an architectural style typified by postwar slab blocks of various sizes dating from the 1950s through the 1980s. Cook's strategy was to provide a series of 'places', or focal points that create areas of activity within the space and to wrap the slabs with a new outer skin.

Ink, watercolour, and pencil drawing of Breitscheidplatz as visualised by Peter Cook

'Design for a Memorial, Axonometric View and Section'

Julian Cowie

Competition 1992

'Design for a Memorial, Axonometric View and Section' is part of a winning submission in a competition for ideas to address the problem of finding a suitable setting for the storage of cremated remains. The design is based around a cloister defined on four sides by a vaulted loggia. The outer wall of each vaulted bay contains a columbarium made of inscribed stone panels, behind which the remains are kept. Between each pair of columns is a seat for visitors pausing for contemplation and prayer.

On two sides of the cloister are semicircular chapels to be used for memorial services and for keeping a memorial record book. On the adjacent sides are two stair towers that lead to the other floors. The lowest level is an intimate crypt that holds another columbarium and is lit by a central reflecting pool. The highest level, in contrast, is an open promenade from which one can view the surrounding landscape and the cloister below.

Cowie's sketches show the development of the design   *opposite:* Axonometric view and cross section

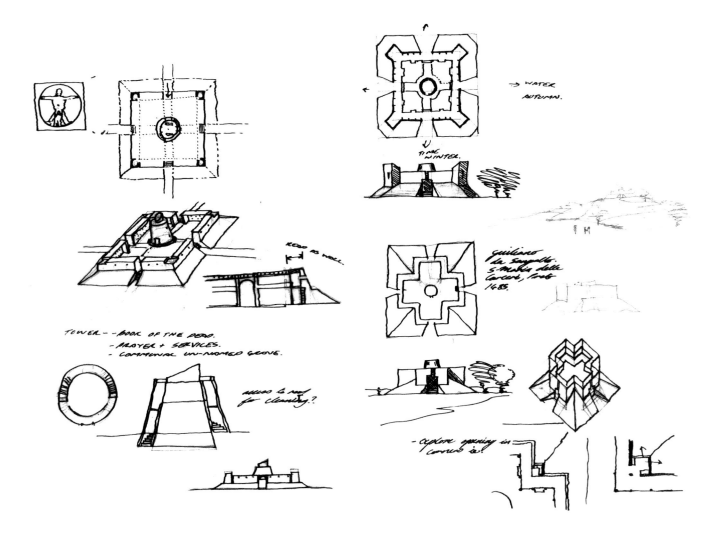

Fountains Abbey Visitor Centre, Yorkshire

Edward Cullinan Architects

Commissioned 1987
Building commenced 1990
Completed 1992
Design Team Edward Cullinan, Alex Gillies, Jonathan Hale,
    Carol Costello, Jeremy Stacey, Tom Fitzsimmons
Client The National Trust
Structural Engineer Jampel Davidson & Bell
Services Engineer MEDA
Quantity Surveyor E. C. Harris
Shop Fitting & Exhibition Design John Herbert Partnership

Section through the Visitor Centre looking east. Drawing by Jonathan Hale

In 1987 the National Trust commissioned Edward Cullinan Architects to design a visitors' centre and a new
landscaped car park at the World Architectural Heritage
Site at Fountains Abbey in Yorkshire, one of the great
twelfth-century Cistercian monasteries. The site is high
up above the valley of the river Skell. The visitors' centre is located on a new approach to the abbey that follows the route of an ancient pathway, originally used by
monks but long since fallen into disuse.

The building is arranged around a courtyard set on the
axis of a view from the approach road to the abbey tower, built by Abbot Huby in the early part of the sixteenth
century. The external elevations of the centre are made
of dry-stone walls under clerestory glazing, which is
protected by steeply pitched stone-tile roofs with over-
sailing eaves. This hard outer 'shell' contrasts with the
softer, lighter courtyard elevations: timber-framed
glazed screens under double-curved, lead-covered roofs,
the eaves of which extend to form a generous covered
way. The glazing of the building's elevations is achieved
by spacing eight-inch wide cedar boards six inches apart
and inserting glass into the spaces to allow filtered light
to pass, reminiscent of the windows of local farm buildings. The building is contemporary yet designed with
respect for its richly historic surroundings and an awareness of the practical needs of the 300,000 visitors who
come to the abbey each year.

View of restaurant exterior: the local drystone walling is
an important feature of the façades. *Photo: Richard Willcock*

The building sits comfortably in the landscape. *Photo: Huw Nicholls*

Petershill House, City of London

Edward Cullinan Architects

Competition 1988
Design Team Edward Cullinan, Tom Fitzsimmons,
  Alex Gillies, Simon Knox, Joe Navin, Robin Nicholson
Client MEPC
Structural and Services Engineers Ove Arup and Partners
Quantity Surveyor Cyril Sweett & Partners
Traffic Consultant JMC Consultants Ltd

Aerial view of the new public space created by the proposed building
Drawing: Peter Kirkham

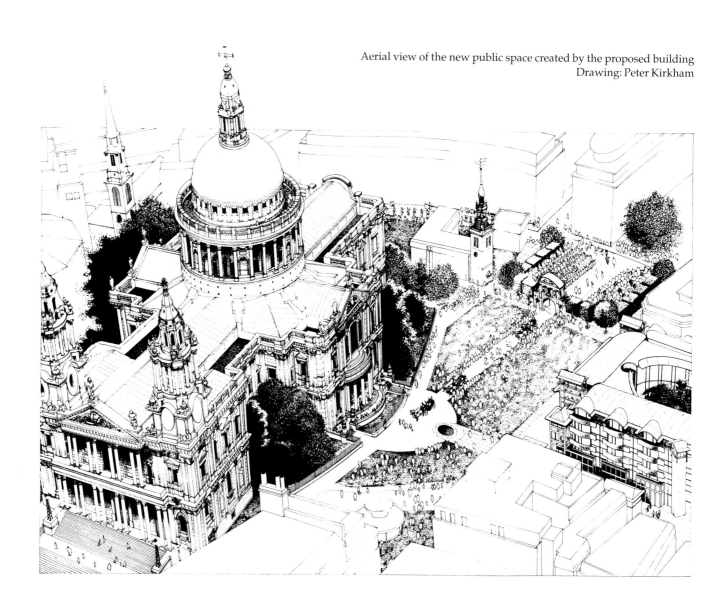

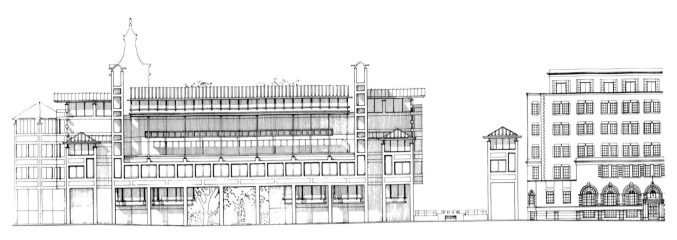

Carter Lane elevation

Petershill House, an office building just south of Saint Paul's Cathedral, was the subject of an invited competition in 1988. The challenge posed by this most public of sites was to reconcile the demands of a contemporary office building with the need to protect the setting of the cathedral and the opportunity to enhance the rich urban character of the City of London. The scheme by Edward Cullinan Architects won the competition, because, according to the judges, it 'suggested the most human office spaces' and proposed 'external spaces, which offered a great variety of interest to the public as well as the office users'.

The proposal attempted to create a coherent public space, one that was conscious of its past and crisscrossed by medieval streets that offered pedestrians oblique and partial views of Saint Paul's and other great City churches. An oval central court would be established to allow plenty of sunlight into the site, and Christopher Wren's tower of Saint Mary Magdalen Church, which had stood on the site until the 1880s, would be returned to serve as a focal point. The elevations would be made of London's great materials — soft red brick and Portland stone. Cullinan studied ways of improving the area immediately south of the cathedral by relocating the tourist coach park and diverting traffic. This allowed the creation of a cathedral green, giving Saint Paul's a suitably grand setting. The coach park was to be relocated east of the green, with the historic City gate, Temple Bar, concealing the coaches and defining the edge of the enclosure.

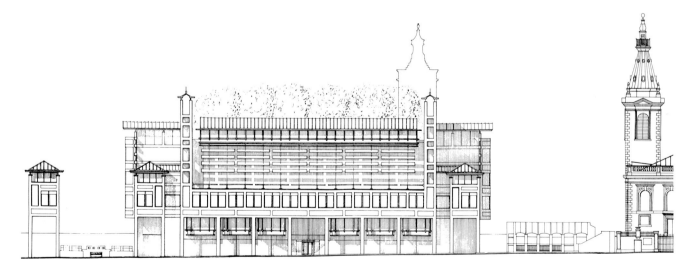

Queen Victoria Street elevation

'A Gateway for Venice':
A new Bus Station on the Piazzale Roma

Jeremy Dixon . Edward Jones

Competition 1991
Structural Engineer Anthony Hunt, YRM Anthony Hunt Associates
Transportation Consultants Ninian Logan, Logan Associates Ltd

Model of the winning scheme. Model: Richard Armiger/The Network. *Photo: Andrew Putler*

Jeremy Dixon and Edward Jones were awarded the Piazzale Roma project following an open competition. The entries and the winners were announced at the Venice Biennale in 1991. This solution organises movement in the form of a circus, a giant turnaround that expresses the cul-de-sac at the end of the causeway. The circle is an efficient way of parking buses. The perimeter provides twenty platform spaces, and an inner radial arrangement allows parking space for thirty empty buses and coaches. In the middle are a cafeteria and rest areas for the drivers.

The circular form arises as a mechanical solution to the organisation of the buses. At the same time it is a spatial idea. There is a distinction between this space, occupied more by buses than people, and the typical urban spaces found in the rest of Venice. People occupy only the perimeter and disperse radially into the surrounding city. There is an empty centre in the plan's form, expressed by the reflections of the sky in a disc of water over the roof of the drivers' cafeteria. Internally, the circular form is clear and uncompromising. Externally, the circle is partially obscured by buildings and a raised garden. The drama of the new bus station comes upon one as a surprise that is only hinted at in the elevations. The new gateway to the city — a theatre of arrival — is the circus of buses itself.

David Naessens's drawing in crayon on brown paper of the circular perimeter of the bus station

The circle is a very efficient form for parking buses

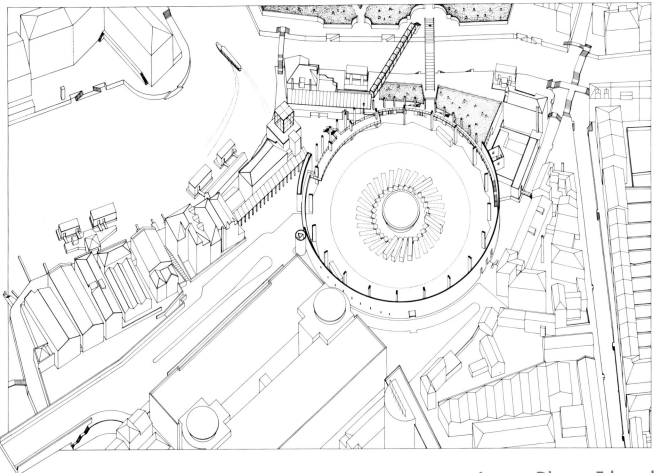

Two new residential buildings for students are the first stage of an expansion programme to be undertaken by Robert Gordon University. The siting and forms of the buildings therefore must fit into a larger idea for the campus as well as stand on their own as individual designs.

The campus will have new faculty buildings in addition to those that already exist. The structures will have the characteristic large footprint of such building types. In contrast, the new residences are slim and elegant.

The residential buildings are located at the top of an embankment overlooking the river Dee. They take the form of Scottish 'tower houses', one round and one square, and use traditional forms and materials. The two buildings are adjacent to the existing School of Architecture and Surveying. The square building has been designed to mask the unsightly precast concrete flank wall of the school's lecture theatre. The circular residence is positioned to take full advantage of its dramatic relationship with the bend in the river. The circular form and the traditional pink finish of the building, partly hidden among the trees, provide a memorable new visual element on the campus.

Drawing of the Round Tower House in crayon on brown paper, by David Naessens

Round Tower House and Square Tower House, Garthdee Campus, Robert Gordon University, Aberdeen

Jeremy Dixon . Edward Jones

Limited Competition 1992
Building commenced 1992
Completed 1993
Client Robert Gordon University, Aberdeen
Main Contractor Morrison Construction Ltd
Structural and Services Engineers Dinardo Partnership
Quantity Surveyor Gardiner & Theobald
Arboricultural Specialist Nigel Astell, Eastland Foresters

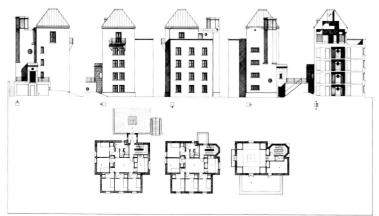

Square Tower House plans and elevations

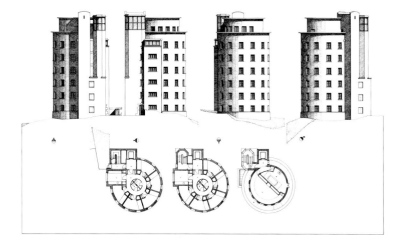

Round Tower House plans and elevations

The canopied arcade is evocative of Plymouth's naval history. Model: Richard Armiger/The Network

Superstore for J. Sainsbury, Marsh Mills, Plymouth

Jeremy Dixon . Edward Jones with Peter Rice

Commission 1991
Building commenced 1993
Completion due 1994
Client J. Sainsbury plc
Executive Architect Elsworth Sykes Partnership Ltd
Quantity Surveyor Henry Riley & Son
Main Contractor Birse Construction Ltd
Structural Engineer Ove Arup and Partners
Mechanical & Electrical Engineer Silock Dawson & Partners
Wind Engineer Professor Tom Lawson, Department of
    Aerospace Engineering, University of Bristol
Traffic Engineer The Denis Wilson Partnership
Planning Consultant MVM Planning Ltd.
Civil and Structural Engineer Ernest Green Partnership

Viewed from the freeway, the local roads, and the main railway line, the site has an unusual degree of prominence and serves as an opportunity to create an entrance feature to the city of Plymouth. The design of the project centres on the idea that a car park can be a romantic landscape, an outdoor room with a strong architectural identity. The proposed form is a grand semicircle lined on its curved side by poplar trees and on its straight side by an arcaded walkway consisting of dramatic overlapping 'sails' developed with the engineer Peter Rice. This canopied arcade will be the largest object on the site as well as the special element of the design that will be visible from a distance when approaching Plymouth along the freeway. It will be constructed of semi-translucent fabric stretched over an armature of fine structural members and will have curves evocative of the billowing sails associated with Plymouth's naval history. During the day, the whiteness of the sail fabric will be silhouetted. At night it will glow, providing a powerful sculptural effect when seen from a distance.
The superstore itself is treated as a restrained and simple brick building. The site is depressed into the ground four metres below the approach road from Plymouth, and the intention is to give the building itself as little presence as possible, allowing the suggestive shapes of the sails to give expression to the project.

Truro Crown Courts, Truro, Cornwall

Evans and Shalev

Commissioned 1985
Building commenced 1986
Completed 1988
Client Property Services Agency
Quantity Surveyors MDA
Contractors Dudley Coles
Structural Engineer Anthony Hunt Associates
Services Engineers Max Fordham & Partners

In searching for a suitable image for the Crown Courts, one that would respond to the location, the architects tried to create a building of unique character and appropriate dignity that would at the same time be unassuming and blend into its surroundings, both in texture and in scale. The goal was to create an inviting and relaxing environment for members of the public using the building, those directly involved in court proceedings and those visiting for other purposes.

Evans and Shalev wanted to design the best possible working environment for both judicial and administrative users of the buildings as well as for the jurors. They also wanted the building to be compact, easy to use – in terms of lines of communication and circulation – and economical in its construction, maintenance, and energy consumption.

The courthouse consists of three courtrooms: a medium-sized crown court, a small crown court, and a dual-purpose court. The main entrance to the courthouse is approached via a covered, gently rising stairway or ramp and is located so as to allow immediate and direct access to all main public parts of the building.

The public concourse is essentially a linear circulation space, accentuated by two waiting spaces – one for the crown courts and one for the dual-purpose court. These spaces combine to form the hub of the building and penetrate the first floor to take advantage of full daylight and natural ventilation. At the same time they achieve an appropriate scale and a dignified atmosphere.

The Crown Courts in their Truro context. *Photo: Martin Charles*

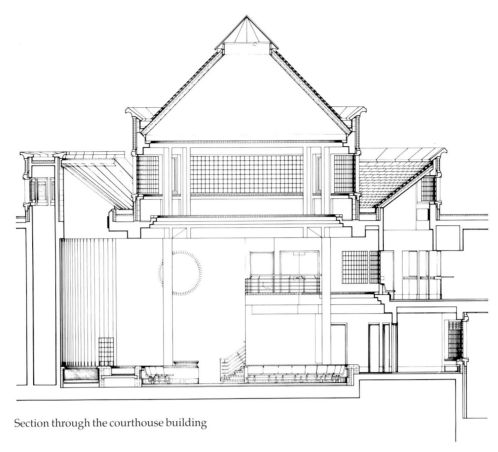

Section through the courthouse building

One of the waiting spaces that form the 'hubs' of the building. *Photo: Martin Charles*

One of the four painting galleries. *Photo: John Edward Linden*

Tate Gallery St Ives, Cornwall

Evans and Shalev

Competition 1989
Building commenced 1991
Completed 1993
Client Cornwall County Council
Main Contractor Dudley Coles
Structural Engineer Jenkins and Potter
Services Engineer Max Fordham & Partners
Quantity Surveyor Monk Dunstone Associates

Sculpture and ceramics on display in the circular gallery space around the loggia. *Photo: John Edward Linden*

Occupying four floors and comprising a number of studio-like, day-lit rooms, the gallery is perched on top of a shear wall facing the sea. The sheltered undercroft for public use provides space for theatrical, musical, and other cultural events.

The building is entered from below. The approach to the entrance is via the loggia, a small amphitheatrical space that forms, once one is in the building, a window onto the Atlantic Ocean.

The art gallery itself is housed on the entire second floor. Five top-lit exhibition rooms are arranged in a simple sequence around a 'secret' courtyard, which is discovered at the end of a linear journey. The visitor follows a route through rooms that are different in scale and lighting. No larger than those of a St Ives artist, sparse in detail, with soft lighting, the spaces allow the exhibits to come into their own.

Four of the rooms are for paintings, each with its own distinct character. The first low, elongated space houses works that provide an introduction to the St Ives school. The second room, circular and hugging the loggia, is reserved predominantly for exhibitions of sculpture and ceramics.

The exterior of the gallery reflects the scale and texture of the town. Like the new building itself, St Ives is a town of white walls, grey slate roofs, and small windows.

The interiors are full of rich detail. *Photo: John Edward Linden*

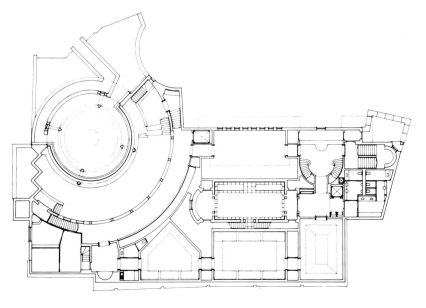

above: Floor plan of the sculpture gallery level

left: The gallery's main entrance leading to the exhibition spaces with loggia. *Photo: John Edward Linden*

below: The white walls and slate roof reflect the local building styles. *Photo: John Edward Linden*

Perspective view of the building towards the south-east

Camden Arts Centre

Feary + Heron Architects

Commissioned 1991
Due to commence 1995
Client Camden Arts Centre
Quantity Surveyor Andrews and Boyd
Structural Engineer Hockley & Dawson
Services Engineer Max Fordham & Partners

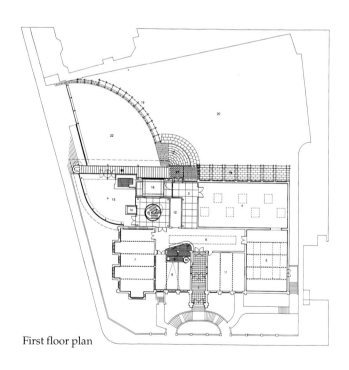

First floor plan

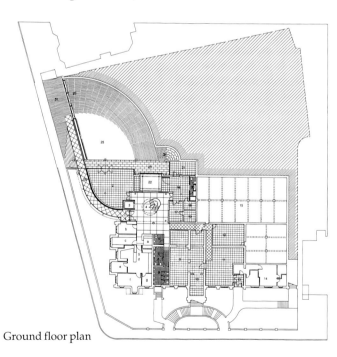

Ground floor plan

Camden Arts Centre is situated in North London on a prominent site at the corner of two heavily trafficked roads. As a gallery it has gained a reputation for a programme that includes both traditional and experimental exhibitions and is regarded as one of London's leading centres for contemporary art. Feary + Heron was commissioned to carry out a study of the gallery and to make proposals for alterations, extensions, and renovations of the existing building.

Delivery of art works to the building occurs on a regular basis; exhibitions generally have a six-to-eight-week turnaround. When not in use (about 90% of the time), the delivery area becomes a sculpture court, visible and accessible from the building, and an outdoor extension to the education workshop. The forms of the sculpture court and extension deliberately take their design cues from the pattern traced by the wheeled movement of delivery vehicles, as the area is designed to accommodate the largest trailers currently used by European art-transportation specialists.

The extension is designed to be unambiguously new and in no way to mimic the pattern of the existing building, but rather to nestle against it. The use of glass blocks maximises the effect of both internal and external lights, drawing sunlight into the building during the day and radiating light from the building at night, revealing a lively and sociable place. The glazed café opens onto the outside in a manner that contrasts deliberately with the enclosed gallery spaces. The elevation to the garden and sculpture court makes reference to contemporary forms and materials, and encourages movement out of the gallery into the garden, complete with new pergolas, steps, and paving.

The extension houses the reorganised internal vertical circulation space, which relocates the core of the building. New features include a top-lit staircase, a passenger lift, and an exhibition-floor lift. Workshop and storage areas are situated on the ground floor, and there is a café on the upper floor adjacent to the bookshop.

The proposed extension matches the original building in scale if not in style. Model: Richard Armiger /The Network

Airport at Chek Lap Kok, Hong Kong

Sir Norman Foster and Partners

in association with Foster Asia Hong Kong

Competition 1992
Commenced 1994
Completion due 1997
Client *Provisional Aiport Authority Hong Kong*
Project Architects *Foster Asia Hong Kong*
Airport Planning, Operational
Aspects and Systems *BAA plc*
Project Management Engineering
    Mott Connell Ltd
Structural Engineer *Ove Arup and Partners*
Quantity Surveyor *WT Partnership*
Traffic Engineering and
Transportation Planning *Wilbur Smith Associates*

Computer drawing of the aeroplane-shaped roof of the airport

The new Hong Kong airport on the manmade island of Chek Lap Kok will provide twenty-first-century airport terminals and concourse buildings designed to meet the capacity needs of an expected 35 million passengers per year in 1997 and a potential 87 million passengers in 2040.

All commercial and core facilities will be built in the centre of the terminal to allow ease of maintenance. Thirty-nine gates will be served by air bridges, enabling new types of aircraft to be accommodated without affecting the day-to-day running of the complex.

Prefabricated steel will be used to construct the frame, which is to be made up of 110-foot modules on a repetitive and therefore flexible and economical grid. The scale of the buildings is enormous. When finished, the first two terminal buildings and the aircraft gate spine will be almost one mile long. The total area of the terminal is 430,000 square metres, the equivalent of New York's John F. Kennedy International Airport and London's Heathrow Airport put together. While there will be 30,000 square metres of commercial space, the baggage hall alone will be the size of Yankee Stadium in New York. In 1997 the airport will have an initial annual capacity of 1.32 million tons of cargo. The architects estimate that the project will require some thirty thousand drawings.

Model of airport building, exterior view
Photo: Richard Davies

Computer-generated view of terminal interior

Cross section

Departure level plan

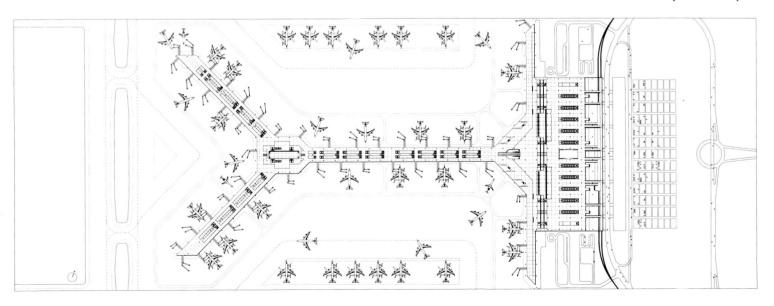

Reichstag Conversion, Berlin

Sir Norman Foster and Partners

Competition 1993
Building to commence 1995
Design Team Sir Norman Foster, David Nelson, Mark Braun
Client Bundesrepublik Deutschland
Structural Engineer Ove Arup and Partners, Schlaich Bergermann + P
Acoustics Müller BBM GmbH, Prof. Dr. Georg Plenge
Mechanical + Electrical Services Kaiser Bautechnik, Kuehn Associates,
    Fischer - Energie + Haustechnik, Amstein + Walthert,
    Planungsgruppe Karnasch-Hackstein
Quantity Surveyors Davis Langdon & Everest, Büro Am Lützowplatz

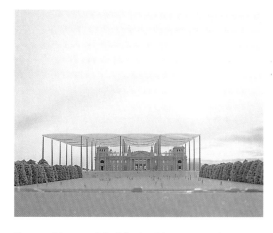

Competition model of the building, viewed
from the Tiergarten. *Photo: Richard Davies*

The Reichstag is an important part of Germany's history and one of the few surviving monuments from Berlin's past. Between 1961 and 1990 it became a Cold War symbol, and more recently it has emerged as a symbol of won German unity.

Foster's winning competition scheme of 1993 for the conversion of the building for the German Parliament proposed gutting the Reichstag and covering it with a dramatic umbrella roof. Foster's aim was to acknowledge, architecturally and politically, the Reichstag's history and presence — rather than to deny it — and to transform it into an integral part of a new composition. The planned structure is intended as a built response to the realities of Germany as a modern European democracy.

The creation of a raised public space, sheltered from the elements, has a timeless but entirely contemporary quality. A podium creates a cloister of new space outside the walls of the Reichstag, linked to new spaces within it. The old fabric of the Reichstag is both demystified and exalted. Our appreciation of the old and the new is enhanced by the visual dialogue between the two. Political and historical continuity is apparent, but the architecture is rooted in the needs of today. The roof creates a space that is open, inviting, and caring — appropriate democratic values for a new parliament building.

The Assembly is located symbolically at the heart of the Reichstag, directly beneath the site of the original dome. Circulation occurs at the podium level in order to connect inside and outside public spaces.

Sir Norman Foster and Partners was a joint first-prize winner in the competition for the new Reichstag. With Santiago Calatrava, and Pi de Bruijn, all of whom were invited to present revised schemes. In June 1993 it was announced that Sir Norman Foster and Partners had been selected as the winners. The firm's revised design makes less dramatic use of the umbrella roof than did the original scheme.

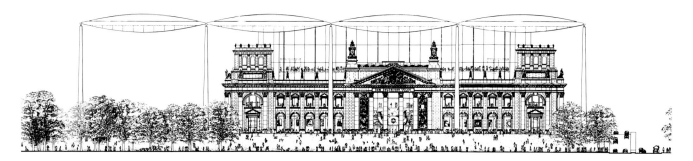

View from the west

East-west section

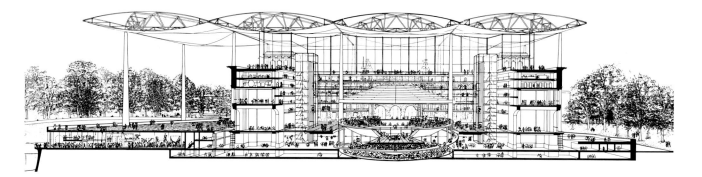

Aerial view of model of the Plenary chamber at the heart of the building
Photo: Richard Davies

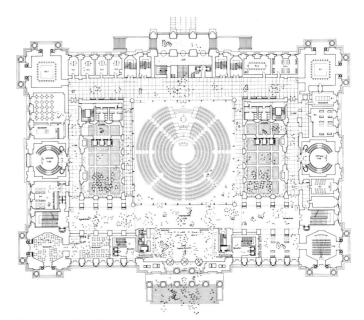

Floor plan of level one

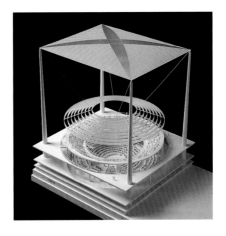

Detail study model of the Plenary chamber
with 'umbrella' roof. *Photo: Richard Davies*

Sectional model. *Photo: Richard Davies*

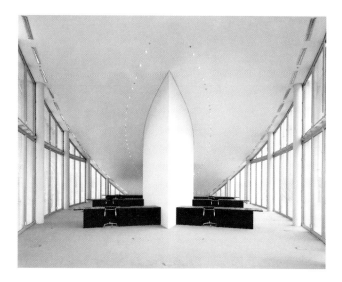

Interior view of the top floor: the lens-shaped core reflects the exterior form. *Photo: Dennis Gilbert*

Business Promotion Centre, Duisburg, Germany

Sir Norman Foster and Partners

Commissioned 1988
Building commenced 1990
Completed 1993
Design Team Sir Norman Foster, David Nelson, Stefan Behling, Mary Bowman
Client Gesellschaft für Technologieförderung und Technologie, beratung Duisburg / Kaiser Bautechnik
Structural Engineer Ingenieurbüro Dr. Meyer
Energy concept Kaiser Bautechnik
Mechanical and Electrical Engineer Kaiser Bautechnik, J. Roger Preston &Partners
Quantity Surveyor Wolfgang Crysandt
Structural Engineer Lothar Schwarz
Acoustics ITA Ingenieurgesellschaft für technische Akustik mbH
3-D Structure Simulation Intelligent Building
Lightning Consultant Claude Engle Lighting

Sir Norman Foster and Partners was commissioned in 1988 to develop a masterplan for an industrial park for microelectronics industries in Duisburg, Germany. The task was to create a centre for microelectronics, positioning Duisburg as a magnet for innovative industries. The site is in the middle of a residential area close to the city centre. The plan is for a flexible building structure that later can accommodate a wide range of companies in the microelectronics field.

The city wanted a Business Promotion Centre on the site that would not only be an office building but also a new landmark for Duisburg, and an urban sign for the microelectronics park itself. The building has a lens-shaped floor plan (50 metres long and, at its widest point, 16 metres wide), with a steel-and-concrete structure, a central core, and a radial support grid of 6 meters. The building is surmounted by a curved steel roof with dramatic terrace-shaped spaces beneath. On the uppermost level is the president's office, with a view of the city. The entrance on the ground floor extends into a large exhibition hall.

The façade reflects the curved shape of the floor plan. It soon became clear that the elegance of the curved level would be lost if a conventional façade with glass support beams were used. The façade ideally should resemble a massive curved glass screen. It emerged that this idea most likely could be realised using glass construction, in which many small glass panels are placed tightly next to one another and then screwed onto the substructure. This substructure had to be able to move independently from the concrete skeleton in order to avoid the need for bulky and complicated expansion joins. Structural studies showed that the most superior solution would be to suspend the façade like chain mail from a ring beam at the edge of the roof. The façade could move freely as its only connections to the floors are moveable dovetail joints. These joints resist all horizontal wind loads. The glass panels, which are floor height (3.05 metres) and 1.05 metres wide, are bonded with silicon.

opposite: Exterior at night: the curved facade is suspended from a ring beam at the edge of the roof. *Photo: Dennis Gilbert*

Typical floor plan

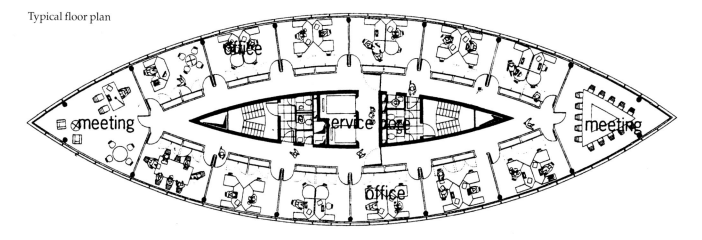

Casino Kursaal, Ostend
Sir Norman Foster and Partners

Competition 1993
Design Team Sir Norman Foster, Spencer de Grey,
    Ken Shuttleworth, Huw Thomas, Max Neal,
    Chris Bubb, Barnaby Gunning, Amanda Bates
Engineers YRM Anthony Hunt Associates
Services Engineers Ove Arup and Partners
Main Contractor John Sisk & Sons

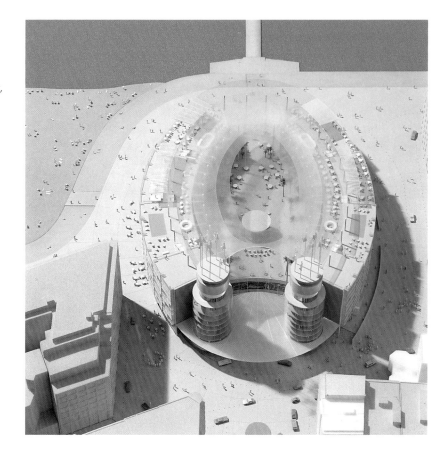

View of model from above. The glazed
roof of the agora rises to eight storeys.
Model: Amalgam. *Photo: Richard Davies*

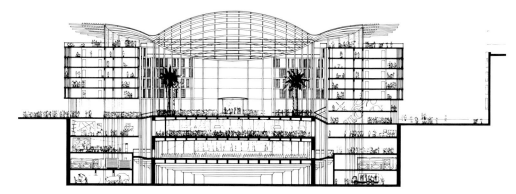

0   25m

East-west section

North-south section

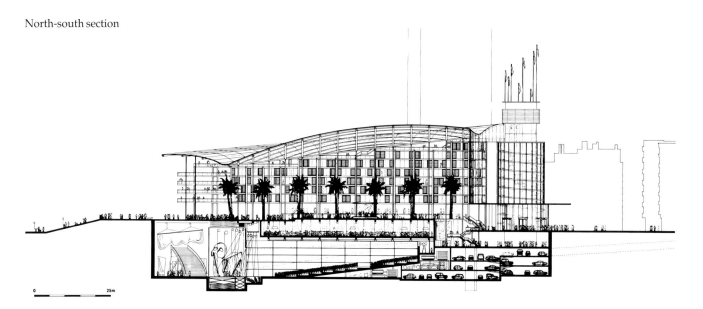

0   25m

Foster's proposals for the Casino Kursaal at Ostend in Belgium are centred around a grand and elegant agora, which forms the focus of the scheme. The agora, with its glazed roof and independent structural support, rises to a height of eight storeys. The arched form of the lobster-tail roof slopes down towards the sea to a height of five storeys at the seafront. Two curved wings enclose the agora on its east and west elevations. Each wing steps down four storeys towards the sea from its highest point at the entrance.

To the east, on the roof of the hotel which forms part of the complex a sequence of stepped terraces accommodates its accompanying restaurant, kitchens, and other support spaces, a bar and lounge with panoramic views to the sea, and sports and leisure facilities for hotel guests. The terraces, open during the summer, can be enclosed in areas during the winter. The structural system provides a high degree of flexibility for the enclosures in order to respond to particular weather conditions. The architectural treatment of the terraces takes its inspiration from the great ocean liners, proposing untreated timber for the floor or deck and exploring the use of nautical themes for the fit-out.

The casino is located directly beneath the agora, with an equivalent footprint. Natural light floods down to the lower levels through a four-metre slot around the perimeter. This enables a perception of natural light to be created during the day through the use of translucent glazed walls to enclose the casino.

Photo montage of the Casino model set into the Ostend seascape.
Model: Amalgam. *Photo: Richard Davies*

Isometric view

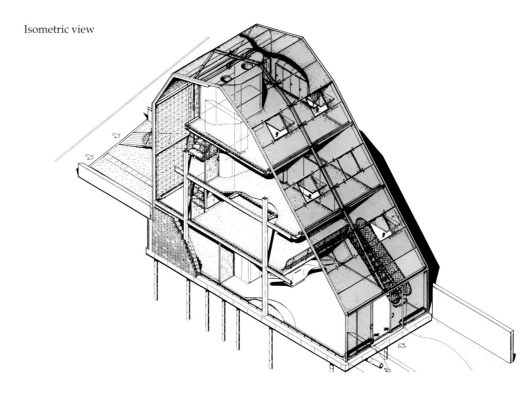

House in Islington, London

Future Systems

Commissioned 1991
Building commenced 1993
Completed 1994
Design Team Jan Kaplicky, Amanda Levete
Engineers YRM Anthony Hunt Associates
Services Engineers Ove Arup and Partners
Main Contractor John Sisk & Son

The four-bedroom single-family house is on a small, narrow site, wedged between the end of an eighteenth-century Georgian terrace and a late nineteenth-century pub. The design takes advantage of the shading and privacy provided by the surrounding listed trees and calls for an almost all-glass enclosure. The front vertical wall of the house features glass blocks that extend to the cornice line of the adjoining porch. From this line the roof slopes back so that its impact from the street is minimised. The cornice line signals the change in materials from the relative solidity of glass blocks to a more fragile skin of clear, frameless glazing that sweeps to the ground.

The structure is a steel skeleton with steel decking and infill gable walls. The gable walls, built from local bricks, form the link between the old and the new. In time these walls will be covered with ivy. A custom-designed aluminium spine beam supports the frameless glazing with stainless steel connections to the glass. Opening vents and sliding glass doors are incorporated into the frameless glazing system.

Circular white ceramic floor tiles are used throughout the house and on the terrace. The bathroom and kitchen units are conceived as sculpted objects and are finished with brightly coloured lacquer.

The almost all-glass structure is shaded by trees. Model: Unit 22

Linking two important spaces in Croydon, at the southern end of London, this bridge provides pedestrians with an alternative to crossing a busy highway via a subterrarean passage. The bridge sweeps across Park Lane in an elegant curved arch from a public park to the Wigmore Hall Conference Centre, creating a daring, reclining structure. The leaning mast serves as a symbol for Croydon, a landmark for pedestrians and motorists alike. The deck of the bridge consists of a series of gently ramped steps, reducing travel distance and making it possible for disabled users and people with pushchairs to benefit from the new crossing. The curved form of the bridge has been planned to preserve all the trees along its route.

Perforated aluminium decking provides a nonskid surface, which drains into the plated structure. The handrails are inclined inwards to prevent children from climbing them. Integrated into the deck is a series of light fittings, directed upwards to create a dramatic nighttime effect. The minimal, lightweight structure has a total span of 113 metres.

The bridge is conceived as an asymmetrical, curved, composite steel-plated deck, supported at each end and cable-stayed from a single inclined mast. Stainless steel cables support the deck on the inside edge only. By angling the mast forward over the bridge deck, the eccentricity of the cables is minimised as the resulting thrust is resisted by the arched plan of the deck. The prefabrication of all the elements off-site and the use of a minimum number of joints reduce on-site construction time and avoid disruption of the traffic below.

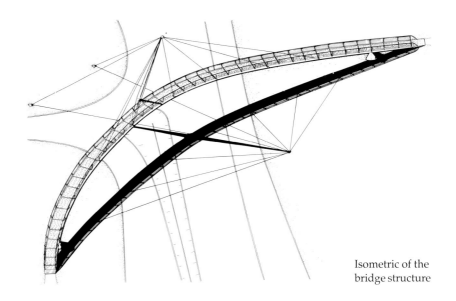

Isometric of the bridge structure

Pedestrian Bridge, Croydon

Future Systems

Commissioned 1992
Design Team Jan Kaplicky, Amanda Levete
Client Croydon Council
Structural Engineer YRM Anthony Hunt Associates

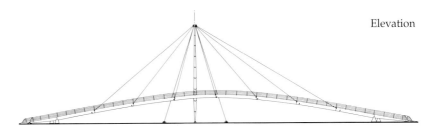

Elevation

Photo montage of the bridge which is planned to replace an underground passage

Stonehenge Visitor Centre

Future Systems

Competition 1992
Design Team Jan Kaplicky, Amanda Levete
Client English Heritage
Services Engineer Ove Arup and Partners
Structural Engineers YRM Anthony Hunt Associates
Landscape Consultant Townsend Landscape Architects

The design for the Visitor Centre proposes a low, smooth glass envelope, all but invisible from the monument itself. Stretching across a wooded horizon, the building conceals the movement of people and vehicles, provides for all their needs, and confines noise and disorder. A thin, raised path, barely touching the ground and directing the visitor to the great stones upon the horizon, is the only disturbance of the ancient plain. Grass banked against the centre creates a continuity between building and terrain that results in a soft contour in the landscape. The building envelope is formed by a gently curved, steel grid shell structure clad in glass. A system of fish-like scales suspended from the structure over three-quarters of the roof area controls the degree of heat and natural light let into the space.

The materials are simple and durable. Glass is the oldest and the most timeless man-made material. It also forms one of the easiest surfaces to clean and maintain. The steel used in the structure permits its elements to be minimal in size and the stone floor used throughout the building is the most permanent surface possible. There are no walls, only partitions that can be rearranged and replaced as required. The structure consists of a double-layer, tubular steel grid shell roof structure, which supports glazing and is founded on a reinforced-concrete ground-bearing slab.

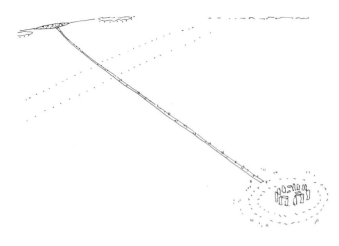

A thin, raised path leads the visitor to the stones

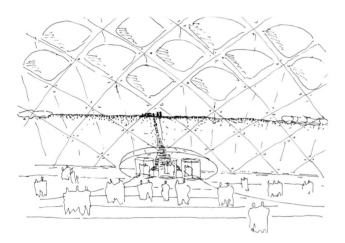

Interior view, looking out along the path

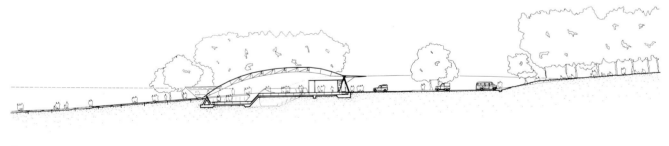

Section

South elevation

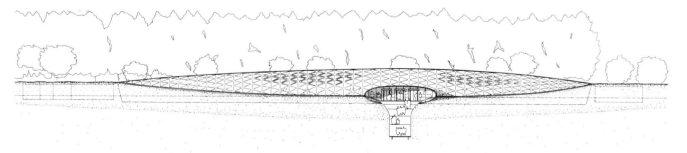

Fish-like scales on the roof control heat and natural light. Model: Unit 22

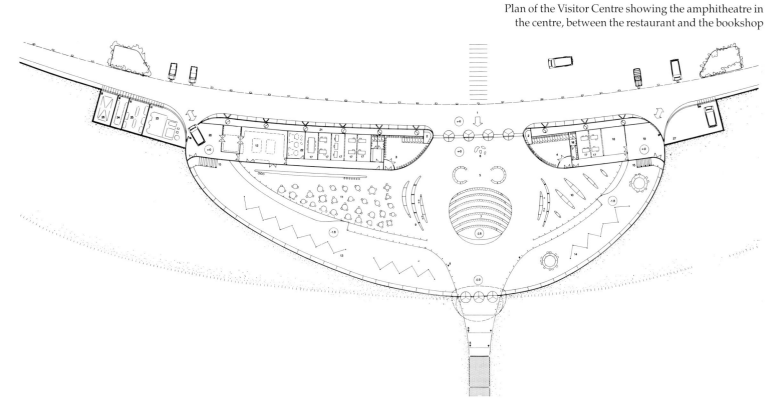

Plan of the Visitor Centre showing the amphitheatre in the centre, between the restaurant and the bookshop

British Pavilion, Expo '92, Seville

Nicholas Grimshaw & Partners

Competition 1991
Commenced 1992
Completed 1992
Client Department of Trade and Industry
Design Team Elon Billings, Paul Cook, Mark Fisher,
  Nick Grimshaw, Duncan Jackson, Andrew Hall,
  Rosemary Latter, John Martin, Christopher Nash,
  Julian Scanlan, Rob Watson
Structural and Environmental Engineer Ove Arup and Partners
Water Feature Consultant William Pye Partnership
Management Contractor Trafalgar House Construction
  Management Ltd
Quantity Surveyor Davis Langdon & Everest

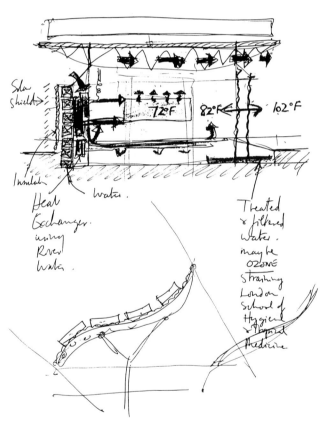

Sketch illustrating the pavilion's environmental control systems

Nicholas Grimshaw & Partners won the commission to design the British Pavilion for Expo '92 in Seville as the result of a limited competition. The completed building retained much of the clarity of the original competition entry. The intention to create a cool, restful haven on the site contrasts with the Disneyesque world of the fair. The white-painted tubular steel structure was designed with no attachments to the ground, and the structural elements are pin-jointed together. The 'kit of parts' construction is therefore clearly expressed. The building's components were prefabricated in Britain and shipped to Spain, where they were erected by British contractors. Only the concrete foundations, ground slab, and concourse floor slab were built in situ.

Grimshaw & Partners used the climate of Seville as the principal generator of architectural form. The structure encloses a large, single volume and supports different types of external skin that respond to various climatic conditions. The east wall faces European Avenue and is the shop window of the pavilion. It is animated by the focal point of the building, a 'water wall' 65 metres long and 18 metres high. The water cools the immediate environment by reducing the surface temperature of the glass, thus reducing radiant heat into the building, and the spray of the water acts on the surrounding air by evaporative cooling.

The west wall shields the interior of the building from the full force of the afternoon sun and serves as a thermal store. It is constructed of steel freight containers — each 1.2 metres thick — stacked one on top another, which have been lined with an impermeable membrane and filled with water. Functioning as thick masonry walls do in traditional construction, the tanks absorb heat slowly during the day and cool down overnight, thus moderating the extreme daily temperature range with a thermal flywheel effect.

The internal layer of the south wall and the single layer of the north wall are made using yacht technology and consist of curved steel masts, spreaders, and rigging, with translucent polyvinyl-chloride-coated polyester fabric stretched between them. This construction allows soft light into the space and fast erection on site, enabling the east and west walls of the building to be completed after the large elements of the exhibition had been installed.

The roof construction consists of a flat, lightweight deck that is well insulated and covered by a single-skin polyester membrane. The roof and the south wall take the full force of the sun's heat. Thus the internal envelope of the building in these areas is shielded by another layer of the fabric used on the north and south walls. The roof shades also support panels of solar cells that power submersible pumps in the reservoir at the base of the water wall. These pump water from the pool to the top of the east wall. By this means the energy of the sun helps to cool the building.

The pavilion at night. Tanks, which
absorb heat during the day, cool
down overnight
Photo: Jo Reid and John Peck

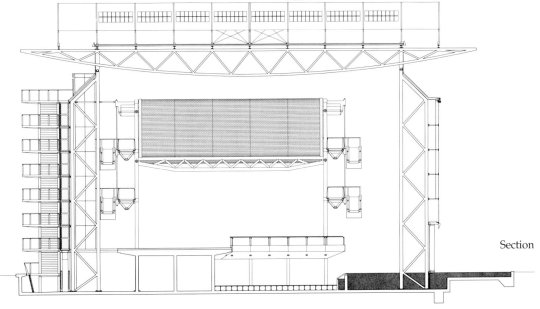

Section

Waterloo International Terminal, London

Nicholas Grimshaw & Partners

Commissioned 1990
Commenced 1991
Completed 1993
Client British Railway Board
Design Team Rowena Bate, Ingrid Bille, Conal Campbell,
    Garry Colligan, Geoff Crewe, Florian Eames, Alex Fergusson,
    Nick Grimshaw, Sarah Hare, Eric Jaffres, Ursula Heinemann,
    Dong Keys, David Kirkland, Chris Lee, Colin Leisk, Jan Mackie,
    Julian Maynard, Neven Sidor, Ulrike Seifutz, Will Stevens,
    George Stowell, Andrew Whalley, Robert Wood, Sara Yabsley,
    Richard Walker
Structural Engineers YRM, Anthony Hunt Associates,
    Cass Hayward & Partners with Tony Gee & Partners,
    British Rail Network Civil Engineer, Sir Alexander
    Gibb & Partners
Fire Consultant Ove Arup and Partners
Lighting Consultant Lighting Design Partnership
Signage Consultant Henrion Ludlow Schmidt
Flow Planning Consultant Sir Alexander Gibb & Partners
Mechanical and Electrical Engineer J. Roger Preston & Partners
Quantity Surveyor Davis Langdon & Everest
Planning Consultant Montague Evans
Construction Manager Bovis Construction Ltd

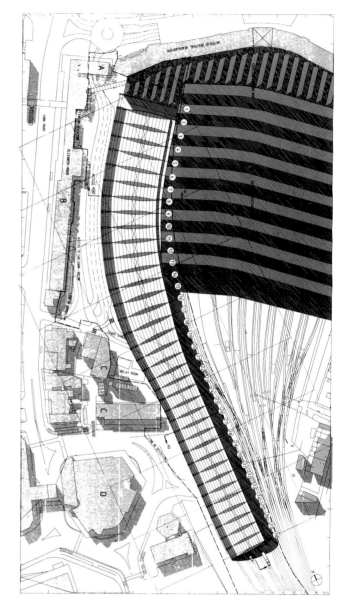

Roof plan: The main station is to the right

Section illustrating the bow-string arch

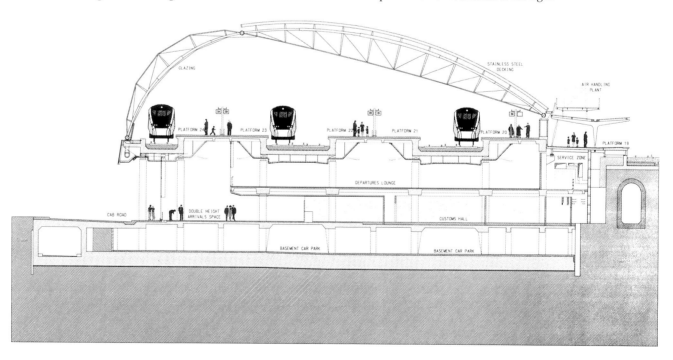

The building is designed as a clear-span steel structure in the spirit of the new railway age. The roof and cladding of the building are constructed of glass and matte-finish stainless steel, which ensure low maintenance and long life for the building envelope.

The roof is a three-pinned arch, with the 'centre pin' located to one side to create an asymmetrical geometry that meets required internal train clearances within the tight constraints of the raised viaduct structure. The structure is essentially a bow-string arch with the cable reversing from inside to outside at the point of contra-flexure to create an articulate and legible structure to the western elevation.

Departing passengers start from a new concourse reached by car, taxi, tube, or train and make their way up a gentle ramp to a new departures hall containing a ticket sales area, shops, and restaurants as well as business facilities such as computers and fax machines. Each passenger-handling zone services a platform with a people conveyor, an escalator, and a lift. The conveyor and escalator reverse depending on whether a train is departing or arriving. Platforms are kept as clear as possible; access for service vehicles is by ramp from a lower marshalling area within the depths of the platform structure.

Arriving passengers will flow downwards from the platform level by means of the escalators, people conveyors, and lifts in the passenger-handling zones. After collecting any registered baggage and clearing customs and immigration control, passengers will enter into a new double-height concourse.

The curved glass and steel roof. *Photo: Jo Reid and John Peck*

View of the building, looking east. *Photo: John Edward Linden*

The dramatic structure is a fitting successor
to the great stations of the Victorian era
Photo: Jo Reid and John Peck

Model of the proposed South Kensington area. *Photo: Richard Davies*

Albertopolis: the South Kensington Museums, 2025

Philip Gumuchdjian

Research project / Competition 1988

Since the late nineteenth century the opportunity has existed at South Kensington to create a dynamic cultural 'quarter'. The rectangular site bounded by Queens Gate and Cromwell, Kensington, and Exhibition roads was originally purchased at Prince Albert's instigation with profits from the Great Exhibition of 1851. Today the site includes a host of internationally renowned colleges, museums, and collections of art, music, technology, and science. It also contains many important Victorian monuments, among them the Albert Memorial, Royal Albert Hall, Imperial College Tower, the Natural History Museum, and the Victoria and Albert Museum. The site attracts some ten million visitors a year (more than go to Saint Paul's Cathedral and Trafalgar Square put together), yet it lacks all sense of place and fails to generate a focus of metropolitan life.

The project proposes an idealised framework for the year 2025 and concentrates on breaking the seclusion of the site by reestablishing its focus on Hyde Park and by sculpting a

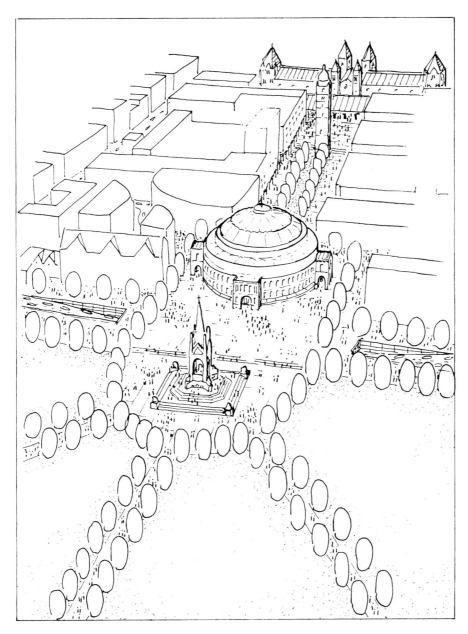

Drawing showing the architect's treatment of the main axis through the site

public realm at its heart. Kensington Road is rerouted a half-level underground. This extends the park's central pedestrian avenue into the site and develops a sequence of three major public spaces following the grand axis of the Victorian monuments.

The first of these spaces, Albert Place (Albert Memorial to Albert Hall), defines the transition from park to city and acts as a focal point for the thousands of visitors to the conventions and spectacles held at Albert Hall. The second space takes the form of a traditional landscaped London square. College Square (Albert Hall to Imperial Tower) makes up the 'collegiate quadrangle' containing the public exhibition and concert halls of the Royal College of Music. The sequence ends in Museum Square (Imperial Tower to the Natural History Museum), which is surrounded by the great buildings, old and new, of Science, Biology, Geology, and Technology.

The squares are accessed through the museums and colleges and are ringed by arcades of cafés, restaurants, and shops, which are designed to animate and attract a larger public to the site. Anticipating the future possibility of the museums staying open late, and the area's busy character, focussed around multifarious activities, the aim of the proposal is to help to transform the site into a thriving international centre of public and cultural life.

The building houses ten linear miles of storage

Hampshire Record Office, Winchester

Hampshire County Architect's Department

Commissioned 1990
Building commenced 1991
Completed 1993
Project Architects Stephen Clow, David Morriss
Client The County Secretary, Winchester
Quantity Surveyor J. Duggan, County Architect's Department
Acoustic/Audio Visual Engineer Tim Smith Acoustics
Structural Engineer R.J. Watkinson and Partners
Landscape Architect Michael Rothery,
    County Architect's Department
General Contractor Waters Construction (South) Ltd

The design allows for future expansion

Some of Hampshire County's great treasures are housed in its Record Office. Medieval charters and accounts, letters from monarchs and prime ministers, court paper documenting charges of witchcraft and murder, and records of diplomacy and espionage can all be found. An ever increasing number of people are interested in the past, and the number of visitors using the building has more than doubled in the last decade.

By 1990, the existing specialist document storage areas were full to overflowing and the public areas inconvenient and overcrowded. The Hampshire County Council decided that new purpose-built accommodations should be provided for this important public service in Winchester and briefed its own in-house Architect's Department to provide a new building to satisfy its immediate and long-term requirements.

The new building will provide almost ten linear miles of document storage for the collection of material anticipated until the year 2020. Further expansion of storage facilities after that time also has been allowed for within the current design.

Due to the sensitivity of many of the ancient documents, temperature and humidity require careful control. This is achieved in a purely passive way by providing massive brick and concrete walls to the north and east that moderate external climatic conditions within the three floors of document storage.

Wrapped around and sitting above these storerooms are the public areas, which are heavily glazed and maximise the use of natural daylight. Sunlight penetration is controlled with a combination of external louvres, overhangs, and internal solar-sensitive venetian blinds, designed to drop and tilt to optimise external views and minimise solar insulation. Ultraviolet-resistant glass (up to 400 nanometres) is incorporated into all external glazing to ensure that potentially harmful rays cannot fall upon documents being reviewed within the building.

Elevation to Sussex Street

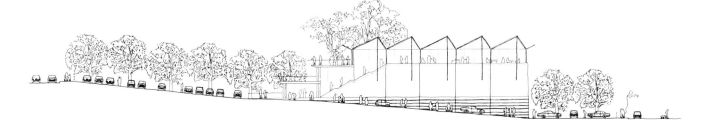

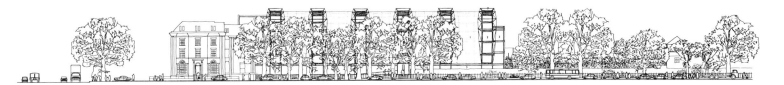

North elevation

Section

Southampton Magistrates Courthouse

Hampshire County Architect's Department

Commissioned 1992
Building due to commence 1995
Project Architects Tina Bird, David Morriss, Bob Wallbridge
Client The County Secretary, Winchester,
    The Lord Chancellor's Department
Quantity Surveyor The Chief Quantity Surveyor,
    Hampshire County Architect's Department
Engineering/Environmental Services Büro Happold
Structural Engineering Services Büro Happold

Model view showing the curved roof over the building's support facilities

The new Magistrates Courthouse for Southampton was designed to reflect its importance as a major civic building within the city. It is located within a sensitive conservation area, which already houses an existing Crown Courts building and an established legal community.

The new building respects the line and scale of the adjacent Director General's House and the distinguished façades of Rockstone Place and Carlton Crescent. The plan is linear, with twelve courtrooms stacked in six pairs on the south side of the site's naturally long axis. The massing of the building takes into account the noise generated by nearby traffic as well as security demands. North of the building, support facilities will be housed in a freestanding unit of consultation rooms, stairs, toilets, and a public cafeteria. The unit has a curved skin of glass and Teflon-coated glass-fibre fabric and is suspended by white painted structural steel tresses. Between the courts to the south and the support facilities to the north is planned a major public pedestrian concourse intended as the bustling linear heart of the new building.

Islamic Arts Centre, University of London

Nicholas Hare Architects

Commissioned 1991
Building commenced 1993
Completion due 1995
Client School of Oriental & African Studies, University of London
Design Team: Nicholas Hare, Jeremy Bailey, Andrew Mulroy, Scott Laur, Lucy Britton,
    Bella Cavell, Laurie Hallows, Sarah Jones, Sam Kendon, Carol Lelliott, Richard Partington,
    Eddie Taylor, George Young and Benedict Zucci
Main Contractor Wilmont Dixon Symes Ltd
Structural Engineer Büro Happold
Quantity Surveyor Madlin and Maddison
Landscape Consultant EPCAD
Acoustics Fleming and Barron

The main entrance: visitors to the gallery pass through the cylindrical entrance space, and straight on into the gallery. Models (below and right): Arup Modelshop

The new centre for the School of Oriental and African Studies at the University of London is designed to house a permanent collection of Islamic art and to host visiting exhibitions. The L-shaped building completes the terrace on the north-east side of Russell Square, which has been vacant since it was bombed during World War II. Teaching rooms are arranged in the five-storey building overlooking the square, while the gallery building, which is much lower, forms the second arm of the 'L'. The permanent collection and small visiting exhibition gallery are linked to the main loan collection gallery in the basement. Above the galleries, at first-floor level, is a walled roof garden and the conservation and teaching rooms. The two wings are linked by the main drum-shaped entrance, which creates a pivotal feature.

Pencil and crayon drawing of the new building which is designed within the context of Russell Square, and completes its terrace, balancing the building at the other end

Ground plan showing the three main elements of the L-shaped building: main entrance block with circular drum, teaching block and gallery building

below:

1 Entrance elevation, showing the layering of the brick and glass façade of the teaching building (left) and the main entrance leading into a circular 'drum' (right)

2 General view from the north-west, showing entrance block with rooflit drum, roofgarden above the gallery building (right) and the teaching building (left)

1

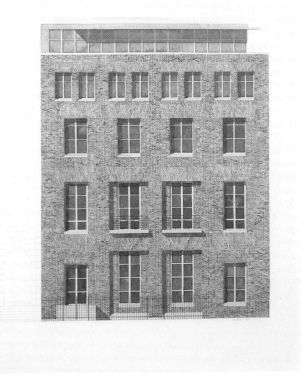

2

Elevation in pencil and watercolour of the new building, which faces east, towards Russell Square

Tea Pavilion, Broadgate, London

Harper Mackay

Commissioned 1991
Client Stanhope plc

Harper Mackay was commissioned by the developers Stanhope plc to submit a sketch proposal for a pavilion in Exchange Square in the Broadgate office complex. The brief asked that the pavilion focus visually on the square and on the termination of the long axis of Liverpool Street Station.

In the proposal, the pavilion is designed as an urban café, a temporary resting place to meet friends, gaze at the trains rolling by, or enjoy a quick cappuccino. The structure and form of the building reflect a dynamic, European trend of conversation and movement.

The building was to be prefabricated in stainless steel and curved glass, its detailing reflecting that of futuristic travel rather than the quiet and supposed serenity of a timber shed. The proposal was not taken further than the initial design sketch and model.

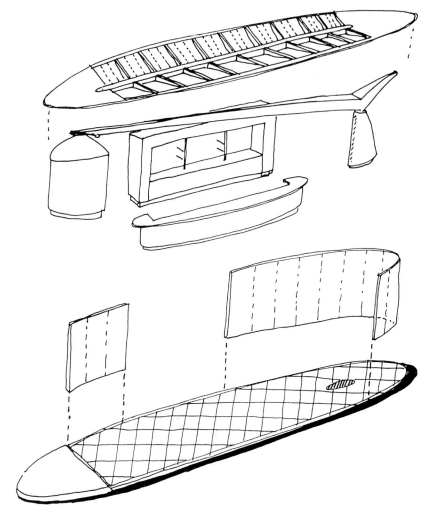

The building was to be constructed from prefabricated elements

The Tea Pavilion was to be sited within the Broadgate office development

The 'V'-shaped roof was supported
on a single column and cantilevered
beam

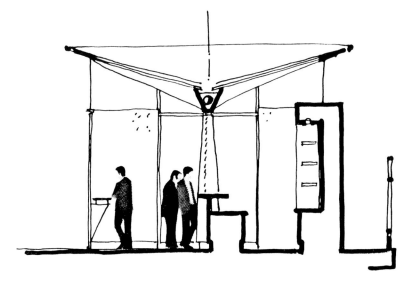

Model of the Tea Pavilion.
Model: Richard Armiger / The Network
Photo: Andrew Putler

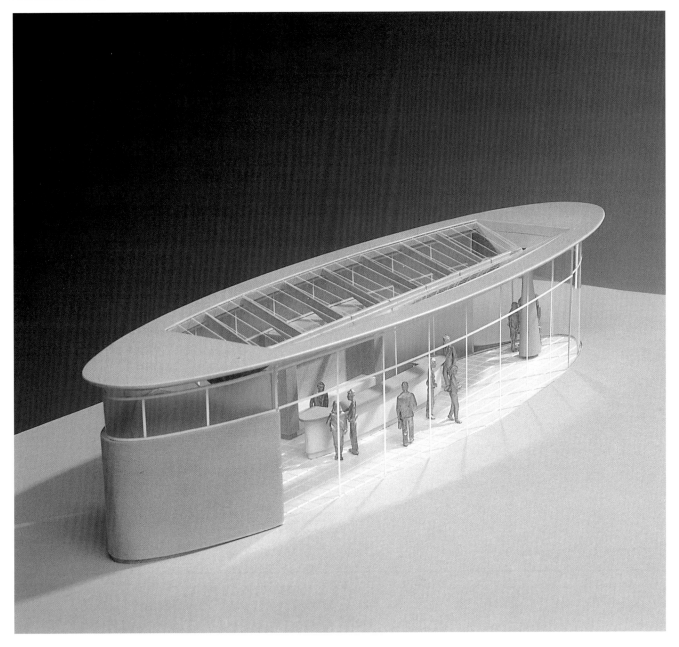

Marylebone Gate, London

Michael Hopkins & Partners

Commissioned 1989
Client Lynton plc, British Rail Property Board
Quantity Surveyors W.T. Partnership
Structural and Services Engineers Ove Arup and Partners

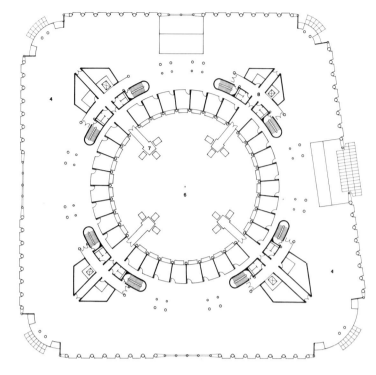

Plan

The entrance frontage. Model (below and left): Tetra

An office building, Marylebone Gate was to have been sited adjacent to the Marylebone train station close to one of the main routes into the city from the west. It was conceived during the commercial development boom of the 1980s but the project was postponed when the market for office rentals collapsed.

The building was designed on a square plan with a large, circular, top-lit atrium in the centre providing the perimeter offices with daylight on both sides. Service cores are located in the four corners.

The strong circular form of the atrium is a motif that appears in a number of Hopkins's buildings, beginning with the round cutlery factory his practice designed for the designer David Mellor, the shape of which was determined by the gas holder that had previously stood on the site. Hopkins's *Financial Times* building makes use of an oval office form and a square central atrium inspired by the seventeenth-century Palazzo Carignano in Turin designed by Guarino Guarini; while in the architects' opera house at Glyndebourne the horseshoe-shaped auditorium is topped by a circular roof.

The atrium

Cutaway model

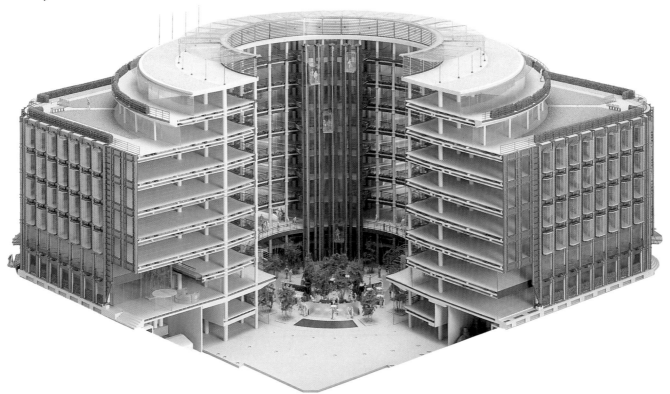

Glyndebourne Opera House, East Sussex

Michael Hopkins & Partners

Limited Competition/Commission 1988
Building commenced 1991
Completed 1993
Project Team Michael Hopkins, Patty Hopkins, Robin Snell,
    Andrew Barnett, Pamela Bate, Arif Mehmood, Peter
    Cartwright, Andrew Wells, Lucy Lavers, Edward Williams
Client Glyndebourne Festival Opera
Client Advisors John Bury, Stanhope Properties
Quantity Surveyors Gardiner & Theobald
Engineers Ove Arup and Partners
Acoustic Consultants Arup Associates
Theatre Consultants Theatre Project Consultants
Construction Managers Bovis Construction Ltd

Glyndebourne is a private opera house, set in the Sussex countryside and adjacent to the country house of the Christie family. The original auditorium was built in 1934 and was extended over the years to hold 830 spectators. The building was demolished to make way for Hopkins's new structure containing 1,200 seats. Among the many challenges faced by the architects were, first, to design a modern building that would sit happily next to the traditional architecture of the house; and second, to create an auditorium that retained the intimacy of the original building. The most striking feature of the ensemble is the lead-clad fly tower with its open steelwork structure. The outside walls are constructed of load-bearing bricks, specially handmade local bricks set in a lime mortar. The balconies and walls in the horseshoe-shaped auditorium are clad in 150-year-old reclaimed pitch pine and the seats are made in plain timber with charcoal-grey fabric cushions. The warmness of the wood and the tiering of the seats creates a space that is at once dramatic and intimate.

The building nestles against the old house.
Photos (below and right): Richard Davies

The interior plan is horseshoe-shaped

Glynderbourne's setting in the Sussex countryside

Wing Tower, Zurich

Richard Horden Associates

Commissioned for the Hochhaus exhibition 1993
Client Architektur Forum Zürich
Design Team Richard Horden, Peter Heppel, Sarah Kirby,
    Sarah Forbes Waller
Aerodynamic Consultant Peter Heppel Associates
Quantity Surveyor Davis Langdon & Everest
Lighting Consultants George Sexton Associates

The tower, a pencil-slim monument sited on the shores of Lake Zurich, is inspired by the forces of nature, air, and water and by the city of Zurich. It turns in response to the direction of the wind and uses the wind's force to help keep its balance around its centre of gravity. The base of the tower forms an island restaurant in the lake, accessible by water taxi or yacht. It features circular terraces and a 100-metre-high cabin, which provides a unique lakeside view of the city. A stepped terrace may be used as a 'stage' for concerts. The Wing Tower is a refinement of a competition-winning design for Glasgow for a monument to mark the Millennium, incorporating aerodynamic lift devices ('wings') to further

The base of the tower can be used as a restaurant or concert stage, accessible by water taxi or yacht. Models (above and below): Amalgam. *Photo: Eamonn O'Mahony*

enhance structural performance and lightness and tilt the tower forward into the wind to maintain its centre of gravity.

The tower weighs approximately 200 tons and is constructed in 100-ton sections, which can be trucked to other locations in Europe. The restaurant 'island' may be retained or removed. Construction materials are predominantly steel and aluminium.

The engineering involves computer monitoring of airflow. High-level anemometers measure local airflow and wind shifts, and the results are combined with general weather satellite data. The tower is rotated to align with the predicted direction of airflow.

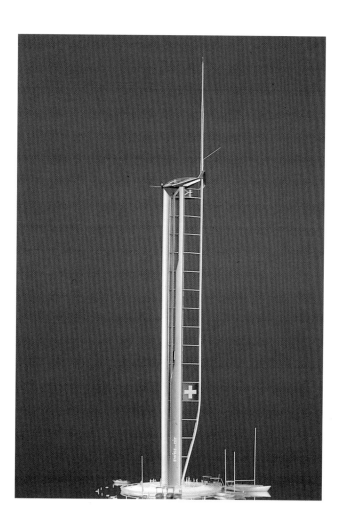

The elegant tower is constructed of steel and aluminium. Inspiration comes from marine and aviation forms but also from modern sculpture. *Photo: Eamonn O'Mahony*

The form of the proposed building acts as a foil to the Opera House, and relates closely to its urban waterside context
Watercolour artist: Vic Carless. *Photo: Eamonn O'Mahony*

Project for East Circular Quay, Sydney Harbour

Richard Horden Associates

Competition 1991
International Ideas Quest Competition organised by
    Colonial Mutual Life — Robert Horman, AMP,
    Mirvac and The Council of the City of Sydney
Design team *Richard Horden, Russell Jones, Brian McClymont,*
    Sarah Kirby, Sarah Forbes Waller
Quantity Surveyor *Davis Langdon & Everest*
Modelmakers *Amalgam*

Designed for the city of Sydney's Ideas Quest Competition in 1991, the prime objective of this project was to create a structure adjacent to the Opera House and complimentary to it, forming a transition between the Opera House and the city. The proposal includes a museum, restaurant, hotel, apartments, and offices as well as elegant pedestrian routes to the Opera House and a new waterfront inspired by the Piazza San Marco in Venice, with water taxis available at the quayside.

The sloping nose of Horden's glass and aluminium structure, which features many shading devices. Model in perspex: Amalgam. *Photo: Eamonn O'Mahony*

The scheme has an intentionally Japanese flavour.
Photo: Martin Charles

Chaucer College is a residential base for two hundred Japanese students at the University of Kent at Canterbury. It consists of two- and three-storey residential blocks for students, loosely grouped around the site, and a courtyard formed by a library, classrooms, a dining hall, a lecture theatre, and a common room. The double-height dining hall and kitchen forms one side of the courtyard. The building has brick walls with clerestory glazing along the eaves and gable, while a narrow window runs the full height of the gable wall. Adjacent to the dining hall, at a lower level on the sloping site, is a structure housing the students' common room and a lecture theatre. It is similar in shape and roof line but has glazed upper walls and gables. The inner roof structure is exposed in both the common room and the dining room. Additional natural light comes from clerestory glazing set in the walls. The architects' intention was to integrate the new college sympathetically within the semi-rural landscape and at a scale that would not conflict with the neighbouring residential properties. The Royal Fine Art Commission endorsed the scheme 'as sensitive and responsive to the site'. There is a flavour of Japanese design running through the scheme, but at the request of the Japanese commissioning foundation the new college has the cultural and educational atmosphere of an English college. Gently curved convex roofs, which in the case of the residential blocks are carried down as tile-capped walls to form terraces, enhance the feeling that the building grows out of the fold of the sloping landscape.

Chaucer College, University of Kent, Canterbury
Howell Killick Partridge and Amis (HKPA)

Commissioned 1990
Commenced 1991
Completed 1992
Design Team John Partridge, Roy Murphy, William Hodge,
    Peter Schmitt, Knud Rossen, Sherry Bates, Sarah Jefferson,
    Louise Carmen, Alison Lufini
Client Shumei Gakuen Foundation, Japan
Main Contractor Wiltshier Construction (South) Ltd.
Structural Engineer F. J. Samuely and Partners
Quantity Surveyor Roger Wenn Partnership
Landscape Consultants John Clague & Partners
Lighting Consultant MRA Architects

Site plan

The buildings
are integrated
sympathetically
into the semi-
rural landscape.
Photo:
Martin Charles

The main
buildings form a
courtyard in the
manner of an
English college.
Photo:
Martin Charles

Restoration of the Banqueting Hall: Knebworth House, Hertfordshire

Donald W. Insall and Associates

Commissioned 1969
Commenced 1970 (ongoing)
Client Lord Cobbold
Consulting Engineers
   Austin Trueman Associates
Quantity Surveyor
   Tapley & Edworthy
Plasterers and Renderers
   Joy Plastering
Timber Treatments
   Bedford Timber
   Preservation Company
Glaziers Kent Blaxill

Insall's drawing describes the work carried out during the refurbishment

The restoration of the seventeenth-century banqueting hall at Knebworth House is the most recent in a series of contracts that form part of a long term plan for the conservation of the home of Lord and Lady Cobbold. The restoration has involved the repair of panelling and joinery, new glazing, the strengthening of the roof, and external stucco work depicting mythological birds and beasts.

The removal of the Palladian-style panelling revealed a hitherto unknown, early seventeenth-century hand-painted archway in almost pristine condition. Also discovered during the work was a man's court shoe, now broken, which had been placed behind the panelling when it was first constructed, for good luck. The shoe has now been replaced with one of today's estate workers, along with a time capsule that includes a compact disc of the Knebworth '90 rock concert, one of the many events organised at the house to fund the repairs programme.

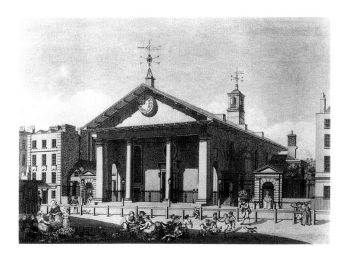

A 1782 drawing shows two gateways on either side of the east front of the church. *Photo: Guildhall Library*

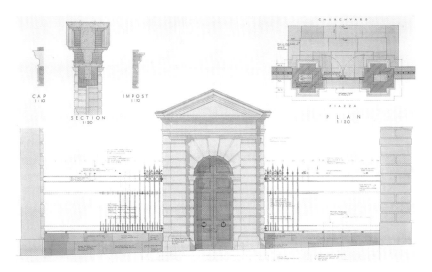

Plan, section detail and elevation

Recreation of Inigo Jones' Gateways, Saint Paul's Church, London

Donald W. Insall and Associates

Commissioned 1990
Commenced 1991
Completion (of first gateway) 1992
Client The parochial Church Council and Saint Paul's Church
Project Team Mark Wilkinson, Jonathan Law
Quantity Surveyor Tapley & Edworthy
Main Contractor Fullers Ltd
Structural Engineer Hurst Peirce and Malcolm

In his celebrated seventeenth-century layout for Covent Garden, Inigo Jones designed the church of Saint Paul, to be flanked symmetrically by twin arched gateways. In 1877 new public lavatories were built on the south side of the church and both gateways were removed. Following the renovation of the area in the 1970s and 1980s it was decided to replace both gateways. The first, to the north, has now been rebuilt; like the original, it is rendered in brick and set with wooden doors. Funds have been pledged to recreate the second gateway, and it is hoped that it will be integrated with the underground lavatories so that Jones' design will form a grand entrance to the convenience.

The east front, with the completed northern gateway. *Photo: Jonathan A. Law*

Garden for Mohammed Mansour, Giza, Egypt

Sir Geoffrey Jellicoe

Commissioned 1992
Commenced 1994
Client Mohammed Mansour

This garden, designed for a wealthy Egyptian client, takes the form of a spiritual journey broken into three experiences that together form a whole: a Garden of Contemplation, east of the client's mansion; spectacular Plea-sure Gardens for the Many, to west of the mansion; and an Underworld below and beyond a Water Pavilion. The Garden of Contemplation is an enclosure of fountains, flowers, and a topiary that is first seen through the pillars of the shade-giving pergola whose colourful climbing plants screen the outside world. The inner garden is mystical, an off-shoot of the garden called the Persian Paradise.

The Pleasure Gardens for the Many are based on a theme of water, which cascades from the mansion and

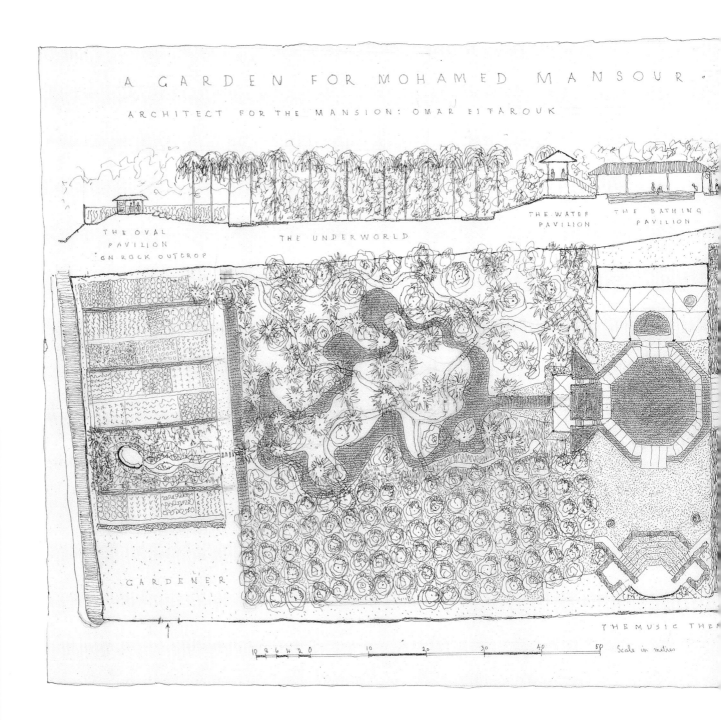

vanishes into the Underworld. The upper terrace overlooks the treed slopes below and commands a distant view of Cairo. At either end is a pavilion from which the mansion, the terraces, the splash of the cascade, and the movement of people can be viewed obliquely. The purposeful visitor can cut through the wild woods or descend leisurely to the cascade level to enjoy the sound and sight of the water. Beyond are the flat landscapes of the bathing pool, the pavilion, and the music theatre. Water gushes down a chute to the Underworld where the visitor may ponder on the first rational efforts of man to survive: the patterns of agriculture that were ultimately to inspire the Islamic art of the paradise garden.

Sir Geoffrey Jellicoe's characteristic drawing for the Mansour garden in ink on tracing paper with crayon

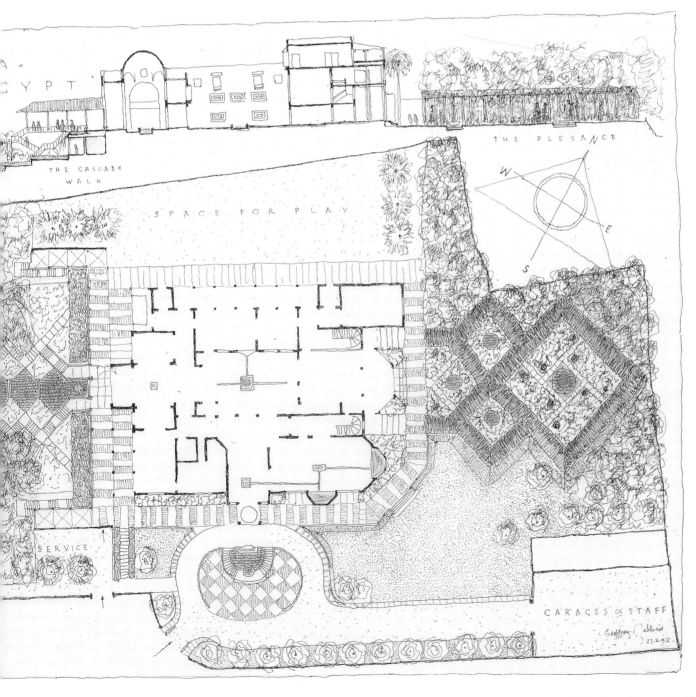

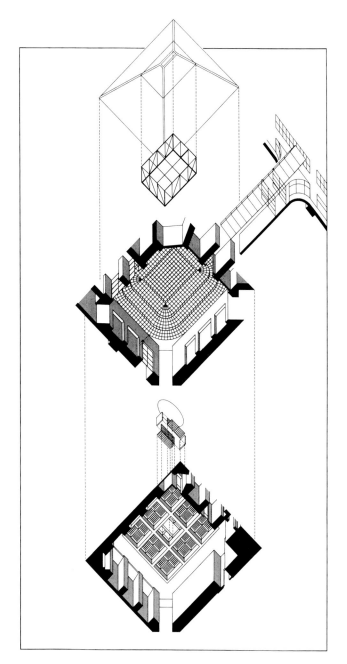

Axonometric

British Council, Prague

Jestico + Whiles Architects

Competition 1992
Building commenced 1992
Completed 1992
Design Team Robert Collingwood, Gill Scampton, Suzanne Gilmour
Client The British Council
Consultants Supmo Atelier 07, Jiri Pomeje
Contractors Pirea/Stamont

The creation of the cultural centre and offices of the British Council in Prague involved the complete reconstruction of 15,000 square feet of the Palac Dunaj, a well-known Czech functionalist building, dating from the 1920s, close to Wenceslas Square. Formerly occupied by the East German government, the buildings had been insensitively altered. The removal of clumsy extraneous details revealed remnants of many interesting 1920s features, such as a glass ceiling in the central space, shopfronts, lights, and a glass-block floor that had been built over. By restoring key original features and carefully integrating all new elements with them, Jestico + Whiles aimed to achieve a sensitive and innovative response to this interesting building.

The focus of the scheme is a large glass table in the centre of the dramatic atrium space, around which visitors sit to read English-language publications and to meet. The table also serves as a giant skylight for the library space below. The office areas are defined by steel screens, locally fabricated from standard components and glazed with white opal and deep blue glass. Unusually for Prague, all offices are equipped with raised floors for a flexible distribution of power, telecommunications, and data cabling.

From the outset, Jestico + Whiles questioned the approach of foreign consultants and contractors who advocated a wholesale importation of skills, materials – and even labour, and who doubted whether the local system could produce good quality results on a reasonable schedule. The objective was to create a showcase for Britain, but the result is also a showcase for Czech skills and for the benefits of cooperation.

Photo: Jo Reid and John Peck

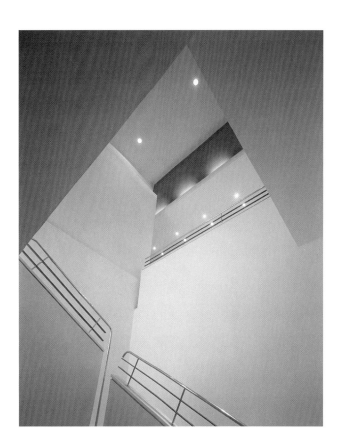

The long glass table in the central atrium space acts as a skylight for the library below.
Photo: Jo Reid and John Peck

Detail drawings of the staircase's
cable support system

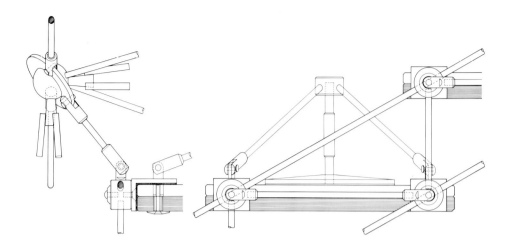

The staircase is the main focus of the interior.
Photo: Richard Bryant /Arcaid

Joseph, 26 Sloane Street, London
Eva Jiricna Architects

Commissioned 1989
Completed 1989
Client Joseph Ltd
Design Team Eva Jiricna, Jon Tollit, Duncan Webster,
  Huw Turner
Structural Engineer Matthew Wells,
  Dewhurst MacFarlane & Partners
Lighting Consultant Isometrix

Sloane Street, close to Harrods, is possibly
London's leading street of fashion retailing.
Number 26 houses Joseph, a prominent
clothing store, and occupies three floors —
basement, ground, and first — of differing
areas, totalling 800 square metres.
A calm, natural quality was desired. A single
element, a simple ceiling trough, was used
to create axes to individual spaces. Each
space was then divided into regular bays, to
be used for showcases for small objects of
hanging systems for clothes. The selected
finishing materials reflect a limited palette.
Beige Spanish sandstone was chosen for the
floor tiles. The walls and ceiling are a
natural grey plaster sealed with a mixture
of beeswax and white spirit; timber ceiling
details are painted grey to match the plaster.
Glass and satin stainless steel are used for
the display system and the staircase, and
brown stained maple was selected for the
joinery.

A mixture of low-voltage and metal halide lighting is used for the display areas, concealed where possible behind the ceiling trough, which also contains the necessary transformers. Fluorescent lighting is used to illuminate the rear of display recesses, highlighting the glass shelves, and behind the translucent glass screens as a backup to natural daylight. Exposed fittings in the body of the shop have sandblasted glass bevels, which give a soft, diffused light.

The staircase incorporates the balustrade to create a composite structural system. Each structural member has been reduced to its minimum required thickness, and the whole system is suspended from the second-floor slab and braced at each floor level. A consistency of detail is used throughout, resulting in a 'kit of parts' to which the various retail spaces on each level of the store can relate in differing and dynamic ways.

Typical Jiricna details. *Photo: Richard Bryant/Arcaid*

Section

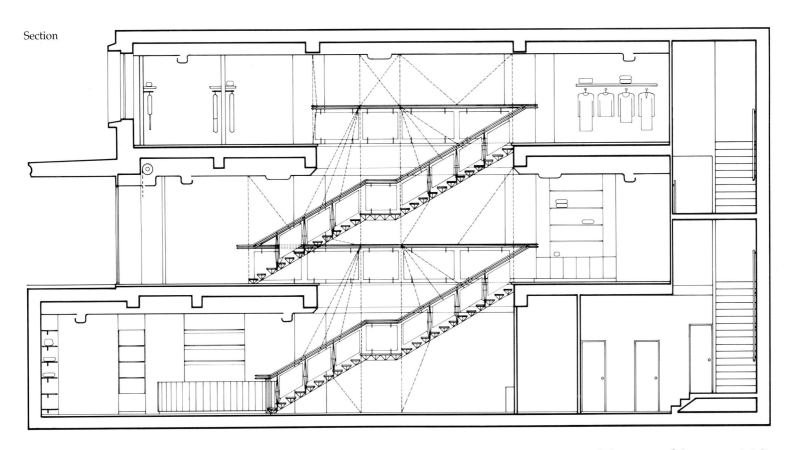

Structural Trees, Stansted. Acrylic on canvas.
Commissioned by Ove Arup and Partners,
structural engineers on Stansted Airport, which
was designed by Sir Norman Foster and Partners

Structural Trees, Stansted / Corridor of Contemplation II

Ben Johnson

Paintings 1990 / 1991
Commissioned

Ben Johnson is a painter who is obsessed with architecture. His subject matter ranges from the early modern, as seen in *Corridor of Contemplation II*, based on the interior of the Dormitorio of San Giorgio Maggiore in Venice, to contemporary buildings, found in *Structural Trees*, the 'umbrella' structure of Sir Norman Foster and Partners' Stansted Airport. Johnson is currently working on a project for an exhibition to be held in the year 2000 – for which the works shown here are the first two works – a series of paintings that reflect a global view of architecture with a particular emphasis on cities. Johnson is not an illustrator or a perspectivist, however; his work demands to be judged as art in its own right. He is only rarely commissioned by architects, and when he is, insists on total freedom to represent a given building.

Corridor of Contemplation II. Acrylic on canvas. Private collection.

Wagamama Noodle Bar, Bloomsbury, London

JSP Architects

Commissioned 1990
Commenced 1991
Completed 1992
Design Team Michael Stiff, Andrew Trevillion
Client Wagamama Ltd
Structural Engineer Lucas Associates
Kitchen Consultant Humble Arnold
Contractor Peter Watts, Charles Barnett

left: Abstract drawing in pencil and pastel on paper reflects the spirit of the interior

below: The interior is a marriage of modern design and traditional Japanese styles. *Photo: Matthew Weinreb*

opposite top: Materials are natural timber, marble, steel and glass. *Photo: Matthew Weinreb*

opposite bottom: Japanese noodles eaten in a refectory-style environment have proved a popular, economical meal

This Japanese-style noodle bar is located in the basement of an uninspiring residential block in Bloomsbury, in central London.

The food served, its methods of preparation and delivery, and the management philosophy of the restaurant formed the point of departure for the design of the interior. Carefully selected economical, natural materials, such as ashwood, glass, and marble, are expressed throughout the interior and reflect the fresh, pesticid-free produce that is used in the cooking.

The spatial sequence is determined by the route from the street into the basement, which has become ritualised by the queues of waiting customers. Surface and plane are manipulated by lighting, setting the stage for the open refectory-type space that comprises the basement dining and food preparation area.

The project explores the treatment of volume, light, and materials – themes that create an appropriately Japanese atmosphere while incorporating aspects of the new modernism, exemplified by an orthogonal geometry and the use of white space and hard surfaces.

Salisbury Cathedral, Historical Study

Andrew D. King

Research Project 1988/1989

Andrew D. King was awarded the Holt Travelling Scholarship for studio design work upon graduation from the Liverpool University School of Architecture in 1988. A requirement of the prize was to undertake some form of architectural study of the student's own choice and submit the results to the school. King chose to undertake an historical study of Early English Gothic architecture, in particular Salisbury Cathedral, the purest example of the style.

The worm's-eye axonometric of Salisbury Cathedral displays both the internal structural vaulting and the external form in the same drawing. The axonometric (scale 1:400) took three weeks to draw by hand with the aid of over 120 photographs. The drawing won a Bovis/*Architects' Journal* Award for a drawing of outstanding merit at the Royal Academy's 1992 Summer Exhibition.

opposite: King's intricate worm's-eye view won him a Bovis/*Architects' Journal* Award for a drawing at the 1992 Royal Academy's Summer Exhibition

Salisbury Cathedral. *Photo: Richard Bryant*

Perspective view from the west (top); short section (middle), and ground floor plan

Ruskin Library, Lancaster University
MacCormac Jamieson Prichard

Commissioned 1992
Client Ruskin Collection Project Lancaster University
Design Team Richard MacCormac, Oliver Smith
Quantity Surveyor Gleeds
Structural Engineer Harris & Sutherland
Services Engineer Michael Popper Associates

The aim of the Ruskin Collection Project, which is based at Lancaster University, is to preserve the foremost collection of watercolours, manuscripts, printed books, and other materials relating to John Ruskin, the influential nineteenth-century British thinker. Because its collection has outgrown its present quarters and urgently requires the attention of experts in paper conservation, the Project organisers plan to build a Ruskin Library in north-western England close to Brantwood, Ruskin's home near Coniston, in which the treasures can be housed and a comprehensive programme of conservation work carried out. In the new building items from the collection will be exhibited to the public in a gallery and made available to students in a reading room.

The protective, enclosing form of the building is intended to convey the idea of a treasury. It stands as an island, a metaphor for Ruskin's Venice. Inside the building this metaphor is repeated in the form of the archive itself, that of a great treasure chest, sarcophagus, casket, or ark surrounded by a skirting of glass rather than water.

The archive provides storage for the collection and offers a potentially stable conservation enviroment. The linear arrangement of the building also meets the need for security: The reading room is remote from the entrance and accessible only through doors controlled by the curators. The plan is deliberately church-like, with the entrance, archive, and reading room comparable to the nathex, choir, and sanctuary. Curatorial offices are located at reading-room level, under the gallery, for convenience and ease of supervision and to allow communication between the reception desk, the administrative office, and the deputy curator. The only sunlight allowed into the building will be that reflected off the sea at sunset, illuminating the metallic soffit that runs through the centre of the building. Ruskin witnessed each sunset at Brantwood.

King's College Library, Cambridge University

MacCormac Jamieson Prichard

Commissioned 1987
Client King's College, Cambridge University
Design Team Richard MacCormac, Michael Evans and Oliver Smith
Structural Engineer Harris & Sutherland
Services Engineer James R. Briggs & Associates
Quantity Surveyor Davis Langdon & Everest

The library combines four functions: an undergraduate lending library, a reading room, a reference library, and an archive.

The archival materials, which include the writings, letters, and other papers of the Bloomsbury Group, are very fragile, and are stored under precisely controlled conditions in massive masonry constructions beneath a plinth. To maintain environmental and security control, these storage areas envelop the reading room, which receives natural light only through a lantern that projects above the plinth and forms a focus for a raised residential terrace.

The undergraduate library, which houses intensively used textbooks, commentaries, and periodicals with a limited life span, is contained in the three-storey independent timber structure at the centre of the building. This structure also contains individual reading carrels for students, and the inflection of its form defines the reading rooms that look out over the garden and sit above the grotto.

The reference library is housed in the layered concentric cells of the curved wall that rises out of the plinth and shelters the lighter structure of the wooden library and the reading room within. The reference library contains classic texts and reference works, together with some volumes from the undergraduate library. The imagery of the library is drawn variously from the ordered ranks of lecterns found in medieval monastic libraries; the synthetic library-garden spaces of German baroque residences; and the tombs of ancient cultures.

South elevation

East elevation

Drawing of the Library by Peter Hull

LIBRARY FOR KING'S COLLEGE CAMBRIDGE

The route through the garden itself is a matter great delicacy, reconciling convenience with the landscape aesthetic. The path is confined to the southern edge of the garden by dense planting which frames prospects of the garden engendering other exploratory journeys and of the building which confirm the route.

The Library is a window to the garden, its entrance framing the longest view to the north west corner.

Ile Seguin – Ile de Billancourt, Paris
Lucy Malein

Diploma Project 1991

The Renault car factory dominated the Ile de Billancourt in Paris from the beginning of the century until 1990, when the company decided to move out of the city and rebuild on a green field further down the Seine. This proposal for the area reintegrates the city's structure within the framework of the abandoned building by focussing on a series of routes and themes that link the site, just as roads, railways, and the river link Ile Seguin – Ile de Billancourt to the city. These include the memory of the former routes to Versailles, which crossed the Seine at this point; the ruins of the palaces and pleasure gardens of Meudon, Bellevue, and Saint-Cloud; the remnants of former industries such as the glassworks, the Sèvres porcelain works, the film studios Boulogne and Renault's Billancourt factory.

The scheme introduces a new lightweight bridge that would link the Ile Seguin and Billancourt. A vast open public square leading to a new Renault museum celebrating the mass production of the family car is proposed for the Ile Seguin. On either side of the museum, a mixed development of commercial and residential buildings and a boat club are planned.

Section study in watercolour and pastel
on Japanese paper and plaster

BOAT CLUB SECTION : LIGHT STUDY 1:50

opposite:
One of a series of evocative works in watercolour and varnish over a photocopy, on plaster and travertine

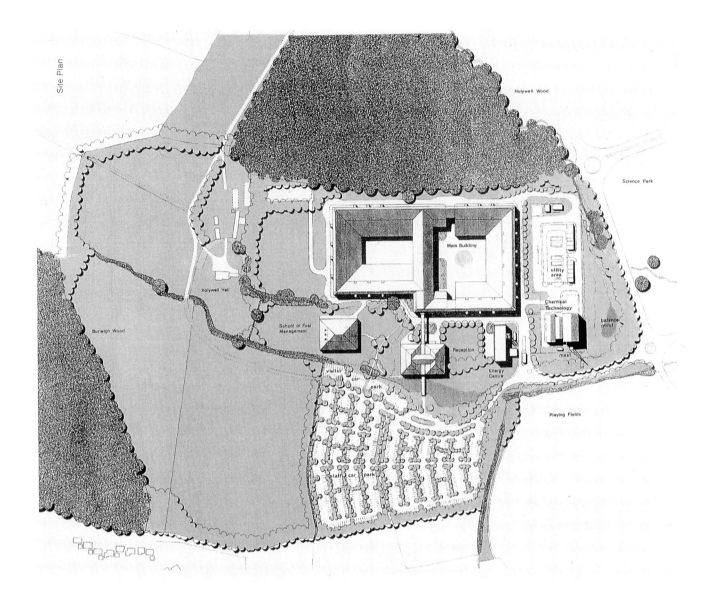

Site Plan

Research Centre for British Gas, Loughborough, Leicestershire

Leonard Manasseh Partnership

Commissioned 1990
Commenced/Completed 1993
Client British Gas
Structural Engineer DGI International

The new British Gas Research Centre at Loughborough is responsible for research involving gas utilisation, gas and oil exploration and production, chemical technology, and environmental issues. The new centre covers 44 acres built within a parkland site of approximately 200 acres. It is adjacent to the campus of Loughborough University of Technology and comprises five buildings. The drawing by Ian Barker shows the cantilevered bridge connecting the reception building to the main offices and laboratory building.

The research centre houses a wide range of gas-related operations

A cantilevered bridge connects the buildings.
Drawing in crayon and pencil by Ian Barker

Berlin 2000 Olympic Stadia

David Marks and Julia Barfield Architects

Competition 1992
Structural Engineers Travis Morgan
    Consultancy Group
Environmental Consultants Loren Butt
Landscape Architect Edward Hutchinson

View of the swimming hall from across the parkland site

David Marks and Julia Barfield's design for the Berlin 2000 Olympic stadia was awarded fourth prize in this international competition. Their concept sows the seeds for a green park linking the city centre and the Tiergarten via the Friedrichheim, the Volkspark, and the countryside. Considered with other projects, this could be seen as part of a new 'green' master plan for Berlin. The principal orientation of the two Olympic halls and their entrances is towards the railway and tram stops. Their forms are soft and curved to maximise internal energy efficiency and reduce the undesirable effects of wind.

The roof of the swimming and diving hall is barrel – vaulted with glazed ends. The vault is created by a system of intersecting self-bracing arches, with double-curved shells spanning the arches. The lower arches from ground to quarter-span are of reinforced concrete construction. The central spans of the arches are prefab-ricated laminated timber with stainless steel stiffening elements and connections. The shell elements, also prefabricated, utilise timber gridshells with timber decking. The shells are connected to the arches to give a structural composite action. The vault is externally insulated and cased in low-reflectivity stainless steel. The cycling hall roof is comprised of two primary forms: a trussed arch that spans the major axis of the stadium, and two aerofoil wings. The arch is a filigree of highly articulated elements that contrast with the smooth shells of the two wings.

The trussed arch consists of circular hollow sections with the top and two side members made of steel. The pairs of angled struts are fabricated from steel plate with cast fittings. Alloy bars stress the two shells together against the central arched spine. The thrusts of the arch are resisted by raking piles or, alternatively, by a series of ties running under the stadium connecting the two ends of the arches. The winged shells are clad with stainless steel sheeting. These are used structurally as a stress skin, working compositely with the trussed beams.

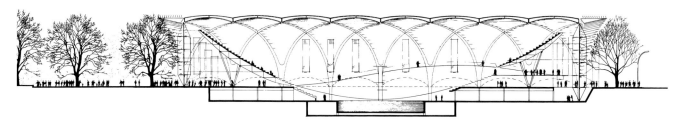

Section through the swimming hall

Section through the cycling hall

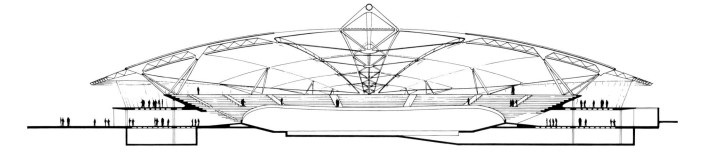

The cycling hall roof

The swimming hall is in the
foreground. Model: WED.
Photos: Graham Challifour

Pembroke College, New Accommodation Buildings, Cambridge University

Eric Parry Associates

Commissioned 1987
Due to commence 1995
Client Pembroke College, Cambridge University
Design Team Eric Parry, Philip Meadowcroft, Robert Kennett and
    Nicholas Jackson
Structural and Services Engineers Ove Arup and Partners
Quantity Surveyor Dearle and Henderson
Landscape Consultants Cambridge Landscape Architects
Planning Consultants Bidwells

Pembroke College is situated in the centre of Cambridge University, and any new building in this context needs to be sympathetic to the surrounding historic environment. Eric Parry Associates' design for new accommodation building for students and staff addresses the requirements of the street while respecting the traditional courtyard plan of the Cambridge college.

The scheme consists of a main three-storey building containing study bedrooms arranged around two sides of a new garden court on the south side of an avenue of plane trees. Two pavilions of Fellows' apartments and study bedrooms are linked to the south side of the main building.

A new Master's lodge is located at the west end of the south block and forms a continuation of the building. It is arranged on three levels and provides space for college events hosted by the Master, as well as private accommodations for the Master's family.

Longitudinal section showing Master's lodge and student accommodation

North-south section

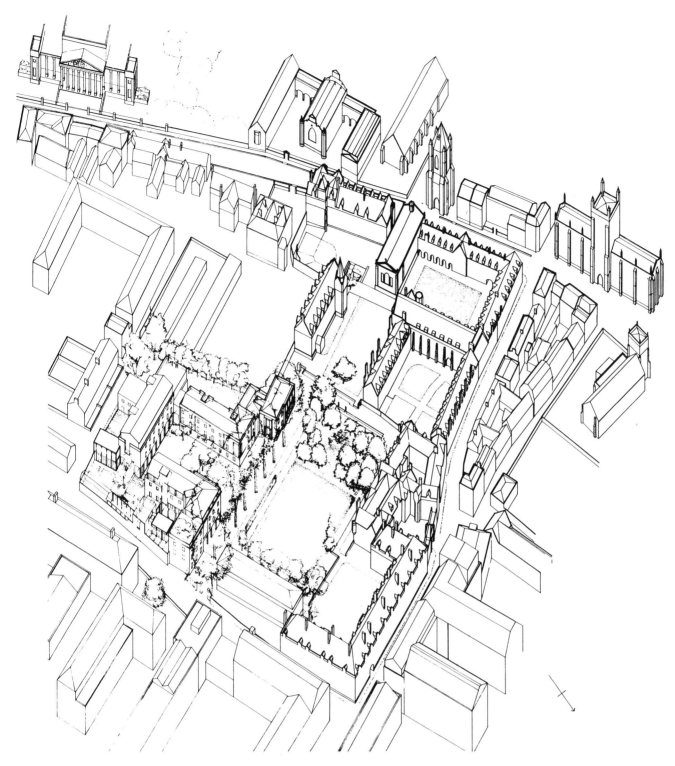

Axonometric drawing of the site: the new buildings are designed in the context of historic Cambridge

Greenville: An Urban Village Prototype

Reid Pinney Architects
(in association with Lyons Sleeman Hoare)

Commission 1991
Client The Urban Village Company
Structural Engineers Whitby & Bird

The urban village is based on the assumption that mixed-use neighbourhoods tend to be more friendly and secure than single-use districts; in mixed-use areas people are more likely to know each other by sight, name, and association. As a concept, it is a development strategy combining the best qualities of the traditional village with those of the denser urban townscape. Designed to reintroduce human scale, intimacy, and a vibrant street life, it is intended to help restore to people their sense of belonging and pride in their own particular surroundings.

The urban village aims at sustainability by providing homes, places of work, shops, and basic facilities within easy walking

Bird's-eye view of Greenville

distance of one another. It reduces dependence on the car, makes for a better quality of life, and helps to ensure a balanced community. The mixture of uses and the close community provide fertile grounds for new enterprises and sources of employment, and an inbuilt flexibility in the master plan and the buildings allows the urban village to adapt incrementally to changing needs. The aim is also to accommodate a range of architecture, both modern and traditional, in line with the strategic options. As a model, Greenville is illustrative of one such possible option in the redevelopment of a particular site, an existing canal-side village with adjoining land in the Midlands of England.

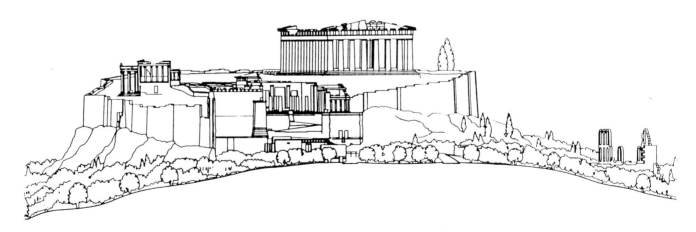

The building was planned to house the Elgin Marbles

New Museum of the Acropolis, Greece

Reid Pinney Architects

Competition 1991

A Museum of the Acropolis, sited beneath the historic hill in Athens, and intended to house archaeological artefacts and an information centre, was the subject of a recent competition. Reid Pinney's entry proposed a complex series of routes, gardens, and structures. Astride a projecting belvedere of rock and stone is a curving shell, hung from an arch springing across the belvedere. The porticoes of this cavernous cathedral of space are enclosed by a light, transparent wall of glass.

The interior, lit by the sky and framed by rocks and olive trees, is designed to contain the famed Elgin Marbles. A vaulted pavilion, accommodating a ticket office and an information desk, forms the museum's propylaea, from which a wide piazza-like bridge, with balustrading created by stone seating areas, provides secure access to a barrel-vaulted, nine-bay entry stoa. To the right of the entrance is the main reception area, the museum shop, and the anteroom to the *promenade architec-*

turale. The *promenade architecturale* ramps up the hillside in three sections; the route is lit by a gridded wall of glass and three spacious light wells. Terminating this ramped route are a central drum of stairs and a lift that provide access to the principal gallery space, the 'open room' housing the Elgin Marbles. Axially aligned with the glazed façades of this 'space' stand the pediments and metopes of the Parthenon. This new temple affords a panoramic view of the Acropolis.

View of the Acropolis from the building

View from the Acropolis

Model

Computer image of the hemicycle, which forms the central focus

European Parliament Building, Strasbourg
Powell Moya Partnership

Competition 1991
Client The City of Strasbourg
Design Team Peter Baynes, Craig Bennett, Andrée Dargan,
  March French, Anne Hulbert, Andrew Jones, Edith Lombard
  Latune, Alan Mitchell, Patrick Monaghan, Jacko Moya, Paul
  Newman, Chris Paulley, Sir Philip Powell, Michael Stewart
Structural Engineer Cundah Johnson & Partners
Quantity Surveyor Monk Dunstone Associates
Acoustics Arup Acoustics
Landscape Consultant Clifton Design
Electronic Consultants The Richard Stephens Partnership

Powell Moya Partnership's entry in the European
Parliament Building competition articulates a complex
of four main elements: a hemicycle; conference rooms;
space for communications (the press) and visitors; and
offices. A major objective of the design was to express
the identity of each element and to give pride of place to
the hemicycle within a recognisable and easily understood family of buildings.
The buildings are designed to take full advantage of the
river and its convex bank. The hemicycle, the principal

Model of the delegates' foyer
Model: Richard Armiger/The Network. *Photo: Andrew Putler*

building, will be clearly visible from both the outside and the inside. Its shape will symbolise its function — that of a chamber in which the members of the Parliament are assembled in a semi-circle around the Parliament's President. The harshness of a this shape stopped by a flat end is softened and given a continuity of form by a shallow curve, resulting in a flattened circle. Its annular foyer is fully glazed so that the chamber — an imperforate cylinder rising out of a glass box — is strongly expressed in a way that can be seen both from nearby and from a distance. It is especially notable from the Pont de la Robertsau and from the road approaches to the north and west.

The four buildings are connected by five main linking spaces: the place — a formal urban space from which all buildings are entered; the foyer — the principal circulation space surrounding the hemicycle, for the use of the parliamentarians; the conference concourse along the northwest elevation; the communications and visitors' courtyard; and the atrium — the space between the communications and visitors' building. In all cases, the linking spaces provide panoramic views and, conversely, allow views into the building from the surrounding areas — a quality consistent with the concept of open European government.

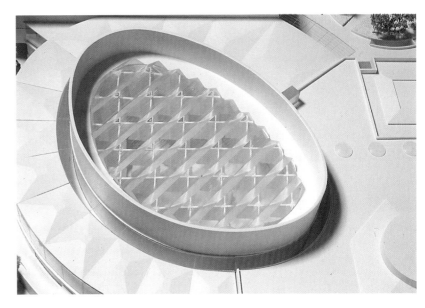

The glazed roof of the hemicycle.
Model: Richard Armiger / The Network. *Photo: Andrew Putler*

View of the complex: the four buildings are designed so that they retain their individual identities. Model: Richard Armiger / The Network. *Photo: Andrew Putler*

Potsdamer / Leipziger Platz: Masterplan, Berlin

Richard Rogers Partnership

Competition 1991

Design Team Laurie Abbott, Peter Barbour,
Oliver Collignon, Mark Darbon, Alan
Davidson, Michael Davies, Marco
Goldschmied, Ivan Harbour, Amo Kalsi,
Oliver Khuen, Swantje Khuen, Andrew
Partridge, Richard Paul, Richard Rogers,
Stephen Spence, Graham Sirk, Hugh
Turner, John Young

Client Daimler-Benz AG; Sony AG; Hertie;
ABB; Haus Vaterland

Structural and Services Engineers
Ove Arup and Partners

The site, circa late 1960s

A major international competition was held in 1991 for the redevelopment of the historic 80-acre site between the Alexanderplatz and the Kurfürstendamm — at the heart of reunited Berlin. The brief asked architects to design a masterplan to transform one million square metres of urban wasteland into a dynamic living space incorporating a mixed-use development.

The Rogers masterplan proposes a framework for a flexible site development and recreates the form of the old Potsdamer Platz as the focus of the historic radial street pattern. The plan addresses future traffic increases in Berlin by offering new public transportation routes and a major transport interchange. The strategy aims for a balanced community on the site — one that includes offices, housing, retail establishments, entertainment facilities, and public amenities.

A coherent proposal for landscaping features a pedestrianised green wedge that links the Tiergarten through the site to the Landwehrkanal. An integrated energy strategy calls for the reduction of energy consumption by an estimated 40 percent.

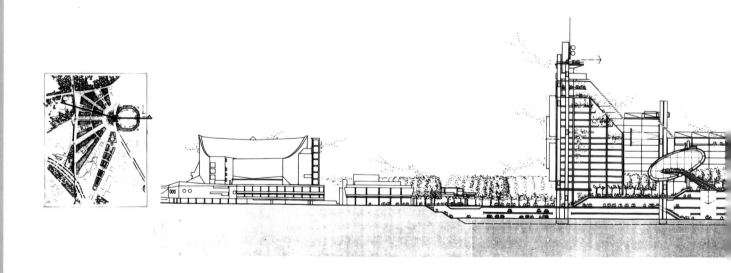

Model of the masterplan. Model: Unit 22. *Photo: Eamonn O'Mahony*

Section looking north through the site being developed by Sony, Potsdamer/Leipziger Platz

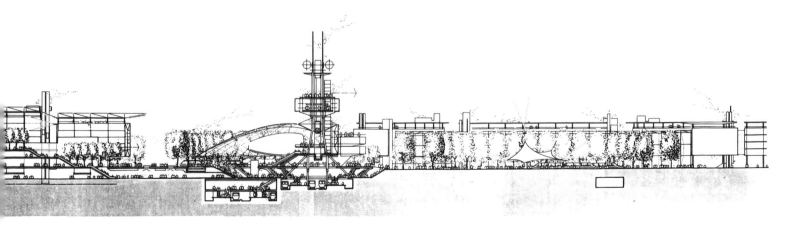

K1 Tower Exhibition Space, Tomigaya, Tokyo
Richard Rogers Partnership

Commissioned 1990
Design team Laurie Abbott, Kieran Breen, Maxine Campbell,
    Mike Davies, Florian Fischotter, Marco Goldschmied, Björk
    Haralsdottir, Eric Holt, Miyuki Kurihara, Stig Larsen, John
    Lowe, Richard Rogers, Atsushi Sasa, Yoshi Shinohara, Kyoko
    Tomioka, Yoshi Uchiyama, Christopher Wan, Benjamin Warner,
    Andrew Wright, John Young
Client K1 Corporation
Structural Engineer R. Umezana
Service Engineers ES Associates / OAP
Contractors Kawada Kogyo

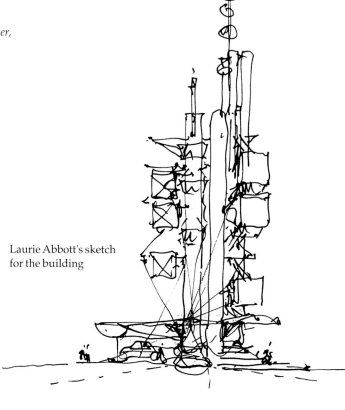

Laurie Abbott's sketch
for the building

Typical floor plan

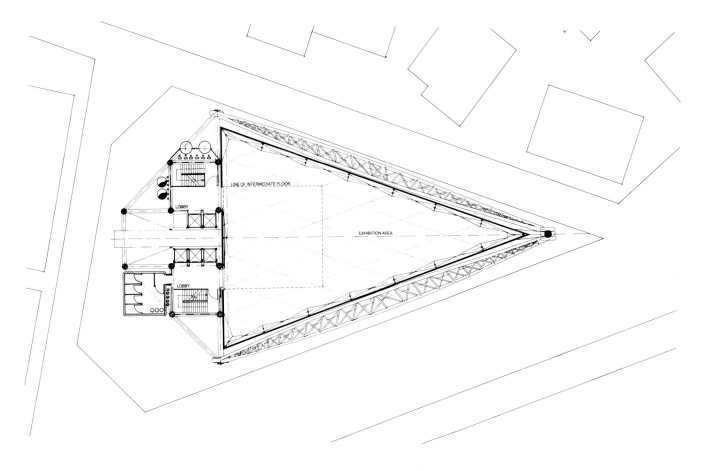

Model built from Meccano.
Model: Tim Price.
Photo: Eamonn O'Mahony

The Tomigaya site, a tiny triangle close to Yoyogi Park and Kenzo Tange's Olympic Stadium, is next to one of central Tokyo's few dual carriageways. It is a highly visible location. Though it is surrounded by narrow streets of small wooden houses, the planning controls that had formerly restricted development to no more than three storeys were changed to allow for the building of a structure 45 metres high, although only the same floor area was allowed. The potential existed for the freakish vertical extrusion of a modest three-storey building into a spire, five times its original height. The architects were asked by the client development company to explore the possibilities of using this additional height to create a landmark structure. They were also asked to consider a design that might provide space for temporary fashion exhibitions. Clearly, image was seen as being as important as commercial viability. A Meccano model was used to explain the ideas behind the project to the client rather than being intended as a specific aesthetic proposal, it offered the chance to analyse the constraints in an abstract way. The three fixed floors permitted by the old density rules would be supplemented by demountable temporary mezzanines that could be inserted at any point on a four-metre grid all the way up the building; the 'floors' could be stacked and stored when not in use.

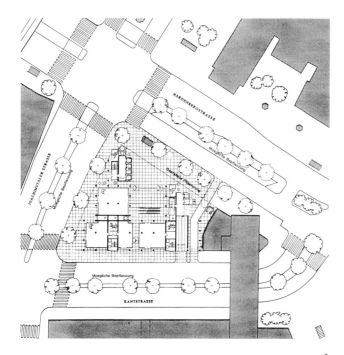

1

Zoofenster Building, Berlin

Richard Rogers Partnership

Competition 1990 (First Prize)
Design Team *Laurie Abbott, Peter Barber, Pierre Botschi, Helen Bruns-kill, Oliver Collignon, Penny Collins, Sabine Coldrey, Tim Colquhoun, Julian Coward, Mark Darbon, Mike Davies, Katrin Dzenus, Karin Egge, Stuart Forbes-Waller, Peter Gibbons, Marco Goldschmied, Lennart Grut, Jackie Hands, Bjork Haraldsdottir, John Hopfer, Oliver Kuhn, Swantje Kuhn, Stephen Light, Naruhiro Kuroshima, Steve Martin, Andrew Partridge, Gregoris Patsalosavvis, Robert Peebles, Cythia Poole, Richard Rogers, Atushi Sasa, Birgit Schneppenseifen, Yoshiki Shinohara, Simon Smithson, Stephen Spence, Kinna Stallard, Graham Stirk, Taka Tezuka, Alec Vassiliadis, Atsu Wada, Christopher Wan, Wolfgang Wagner, Megan Williams, Andrew Wright, John Young*
Client *Brau und Brunnen AG*
Structural Engineer *Ove Arup and Partners*
Service Engineers *YRME, Schmitt Reuter*
Quantity Surveyor *ECE*

3

2

The Zoofenster ('window on the zoo') Building for Brau und Brunnen AG is located between the Zoologischer Garten train station, one of the most important points of entry into the united city of Berlin, and the commercial area alongside the Kurfürstendamm. The site is part of an area of complex overlapping urban layers. Tightly structured streets meet with the free-flowing open space of the park.

The design responds to the pivotal points of the site both as the centre of an important pedestrian circulation system and a key landmark on the Berlin skyline. The proposal is currently the tallest building planned for Berlin, with a public viewing gallery on its uppermost floor. The mixed-use brief has evolved into a building with a public atrium containing retail, hotel, and conference facilities at its base and offices above. The two service towers occupy important positions on the site and create a dynamic silhouette.

1 Site plan
2 The public viewing gallery close to the top of the building
   Model: Jackie Hands/Richard Rogers Partnership Model
   shop. *Photo: Eamonn O'Mahony*
3 Perspective sketch of the extended concept for the site
4 Exploded structural details, showing axonometric of
   relationship with flank and north wall glazing
5 Main entrance. *Photo: Eamonn O'Mahony*
6 East elevation
7 View of the building in model form from the Bahnhof Zoo.
   Photo: Eamonn O'Mahony

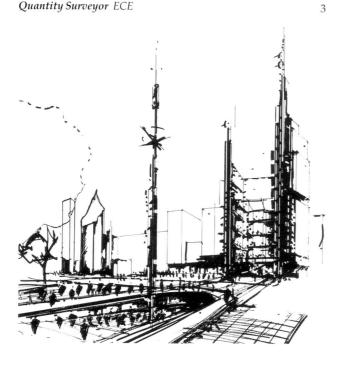

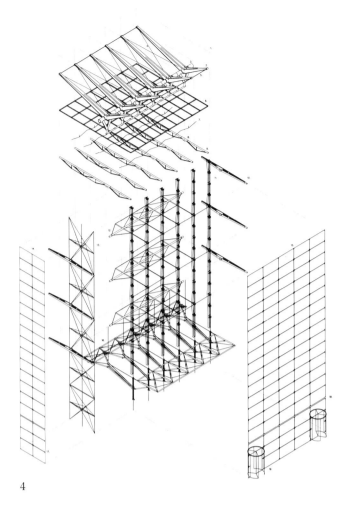

4

5

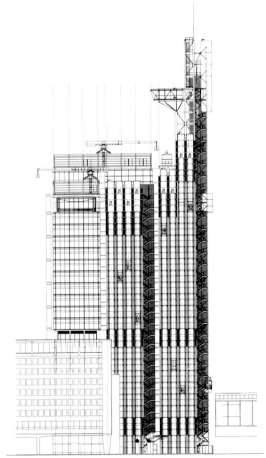

6

7

Thai Fish Restaurant, Tokyo

Peter Salter

Commissioned 1991
Client Toyo Ito

The restaurant was to be located on the plaza level of a newly constructed leisure complex on the outskirts of Tokyo. The plaza steps down from a high-level railway; within this context, the restaurant was conceived as a place to pause between work and home.

The threshold of the restaurant is defined by a continuous bench-shaped form containing the entrance lobbies, fish display areas, and cold storage. A fretted edge allows glimpses of the interior reception platform — from which diners proceed to their tables — and bridges the end-grain timber block and terracotta of the sub-floor and the drainage channels. Sunlight is channelled to the platform from a 'snorkel' in the plaza above. On the surface the snorkel looks like a pavilion for outside dining. Zinc sheeting is used to line both the platform and the pavilion surfaces that show wear, such as counter-tops, screens, and tables.

Located on the periphery of the main dining areas are two private dining 'vessels'. These large-scale pieces, which hold specially designed chairs and tables, were inspired by the rounded volcanic hill on the horizon. Like the snorkels, they are constructed of cold-moulded laminated timber, using boat-building techniques. Each element was then finished by Thai boat-builders, using brightly coloured paint and traditional motifs.

The restaurant highlights the theatrical qualities of dining, revealing every aspect of the ritual, including the choosing of the fish and its preparation in the kitchen.

Ink and watercolour drawings of:

the restaurant, looking across the fish display area back towards the entrance (above)

view between the two dining 'vessels' (below)

interior of private dining 'vessel' (right)

Study for an Architectural Monument, Malta

Michael Sandle

Watercolour 1991

This study for a hypothetical monument is based
loosely on a number of ideas that surfaced during the
course of designing a memorial to the Siege of Malta
(World War II), which now stands at the entrance to
the Grand Harbour of Valletta. Sandle has transposed
the setting to that of an imaginary big city.

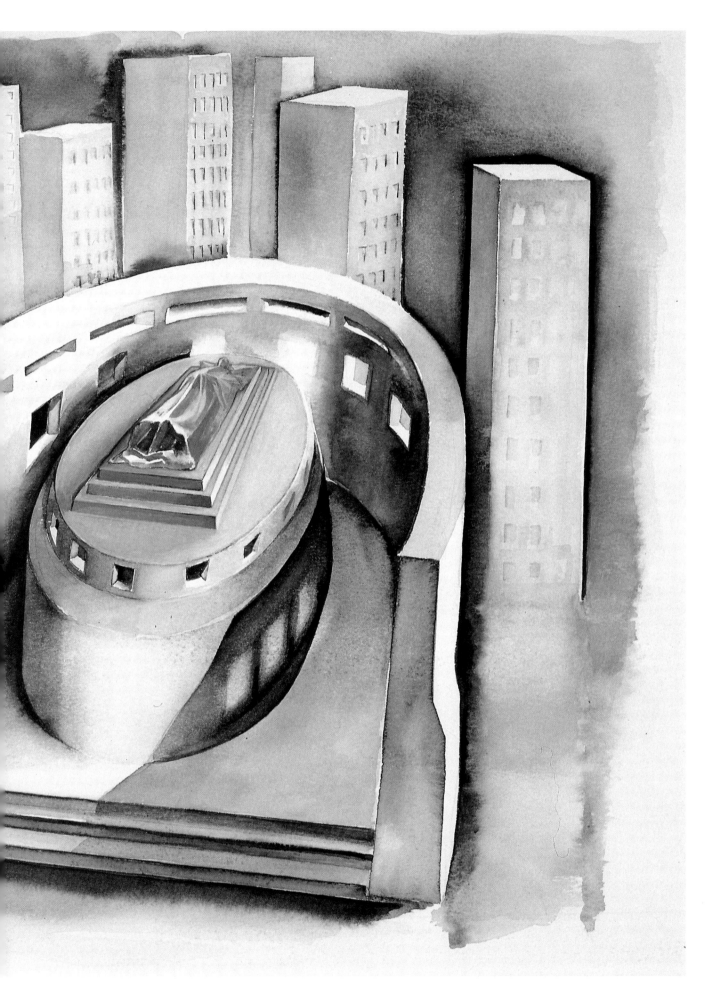

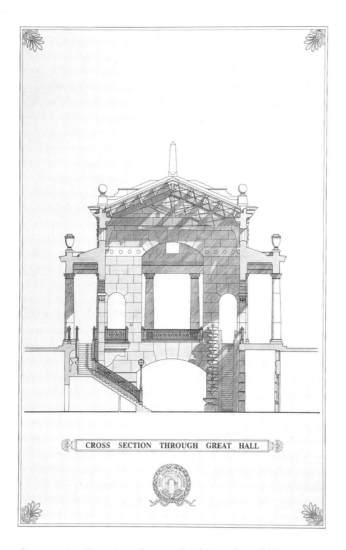

Cross section. Drawings above and right in coloured ink on paper

The New Market Building, Paternoster Square, London
John Simpson & Partners

Commission 1990
Client Paternoster Associates
Quantity Surveyors V. J. Mendoza & Partners
Structural Engineer Waterman Partnership
Services Engineers Janos Baum and Bolles Ltd

John Simpson originally proposed his masterplan for the vicinity of Saint Paul's in 1985. The aims of his plan are to emphasise the need for a consistent approach to the area surrounding the cathedral; to propose that next to Saint Paul's, a building in a traditional style is the most appropriate; and to demonstrate that a traditional approach to planning and architecture can satisfy contemporary commercial, functional, and technical criteria.

The masterplan divides the site into a series of urban blocks, creating streets and squares in the traditional manner. These new blocks have been designed to respond to contemporary commercial and functional requirements in terms of depth and size, but they also relate to the old London street pattern and the historical hierarchy between public and private buildings.

Section

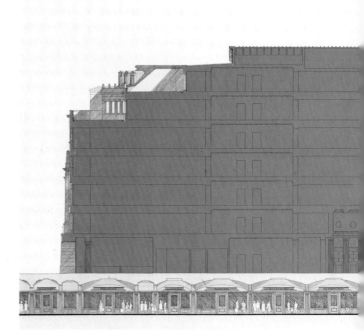

Model of the Market Building:
view of front elevation.
Photo: Jo Reid and John Peck

Front and side elevations of the Market
Building. *Photo: Jo Reid and John Peck*

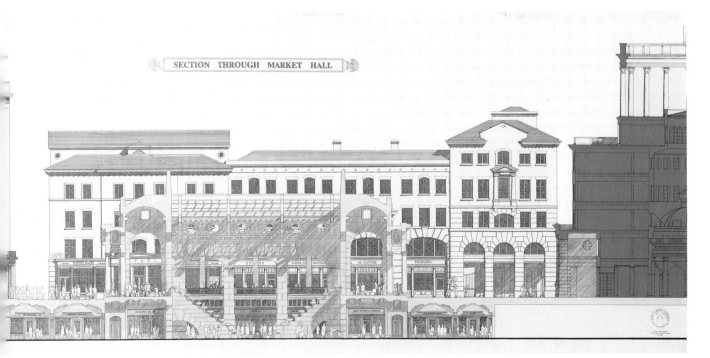

SECTION THROUGH MARKET HALL

The Festival of Britain: 40 Years On

Neil Southard, Alex Ritchie and Ian MacDuff

Drawings prepared for an exhibition held at the
Royal Institute of British Architects 1991
Collaborators *Henrietta Cooper, Karoline Newman,*
   Madelaine Cooper

This project involved the mammoth task of redrawing
all of the forty-two buildings and structures that comprised the architectural elements of the Festival of
Britain held in 1951. The Festival had been designed to
encourage a sense of optimism among the British people
after the dismal war years. Working from often incom-
plete faded general-arrangement drawings, photographs, and sketches, Southard, Ritchie and MacDuff
managed to piece together a lasting record of the event.
The drawings formed an exhibition that coincided with
the fortieth anniversary of the Festival and was greeted
with much enthusiasm and surprise, as this was the first
time many of the surviving architects had seen their
work translated into presentation drawings. The aim of
the exhibition was to inspire new generations with the
same excitement and spirit that had encompassed the
Festival of Britain; indeed the exhibition was seen as a
springboard for discussions of the Millennium celebrations.

The group believes that, as in 1951, the opportunity
currently exists to develop an architecture that is uplift-
ing, innovative and important. The architecture of the
Millennium should be created for public use and liber-
ated from the usual commercial constraints, while
enjoying critical acclaim. It should also endure as a
worthwhile and permanent social investment.

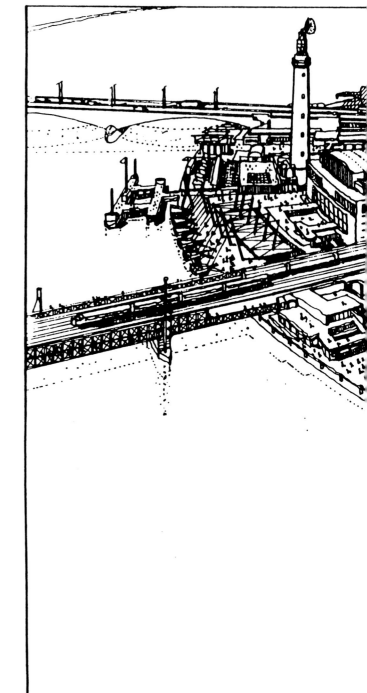

2

1

1   1951 photograph of the Festival site shows the Skylon
    tower to the right of the Dome of Discovery

2   Sketch of the Festival site on London's South Bank

3/4 Elevation and section prepared by the team of the Royal
Festival Hall, the only permanent building of those erected
for the Festival in 1951, designed by Robert Matthew, J. Leslie
Martin, Edwin Williams and Peter Moro

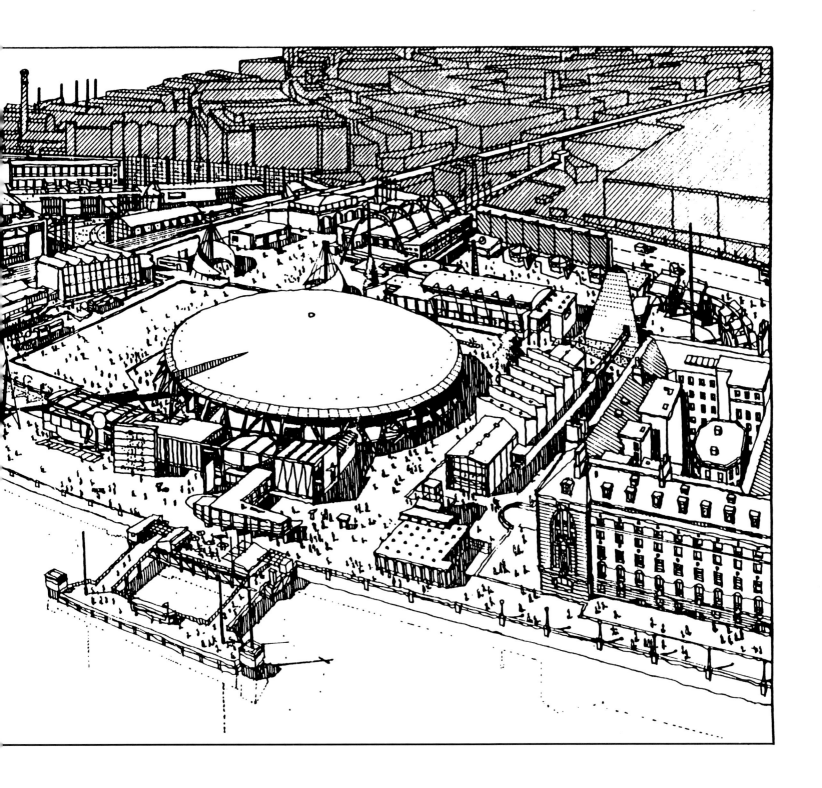

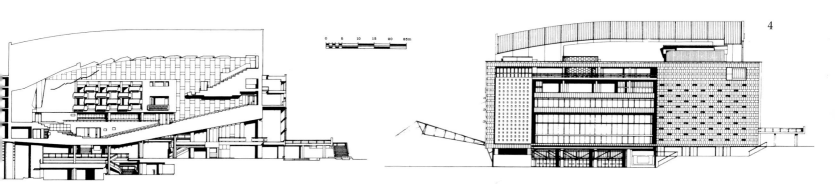

4

Kyoto Centre, Japan

James Stirling Michael Wilford and Associates

in association with
Mitsubishi Estates

Competition 1991

Kyoto Centre, the planned redevelopment of Kyoto Station and its flanking sites, forms a threshold between the traditional northern city of Kyoto, surrounded by hills to the east and west, and Technological City, to be built to the south. The architects propose symbolic and functional gateways leading to public crossings over the barrier of the railway tracks that presently divides the city centre into two halves.

The design includes a new public plaza linked to a shop-lined bridge, which would span the tracks connecting the northern and southern sectors of the city.
A new hotel, arranged as a tower of geometric forms, is placed at the western end of the square. Together with the existing television tower and an oval plaza, it establishes a triangle of civic elements around the square. The hotel silhouette locates the city centre when viewed from the temples and gardens in the surrounding hills.

The station concourse is positioned between the hotel tower and a department store. The department store rises ten floors above ground, minimising its footprint and maximising the area of the public plaza.

A double-height basement shopping 'street' provides a linear connection between the existing subway station and the Japanese Railway station concourse. This acts as a spine for the new underground shopping centre and connects to existing basement shopping areas. A high-speed people mover suspended in the 'street' provides quick access for subway and railway passengers travelling the length of the development. The people mover makes a number of stops from which passengers can proceed to the hotel, the station concourse, the department store, the underground shopping areas, the subway station or the oval plaza.

The new public plaza

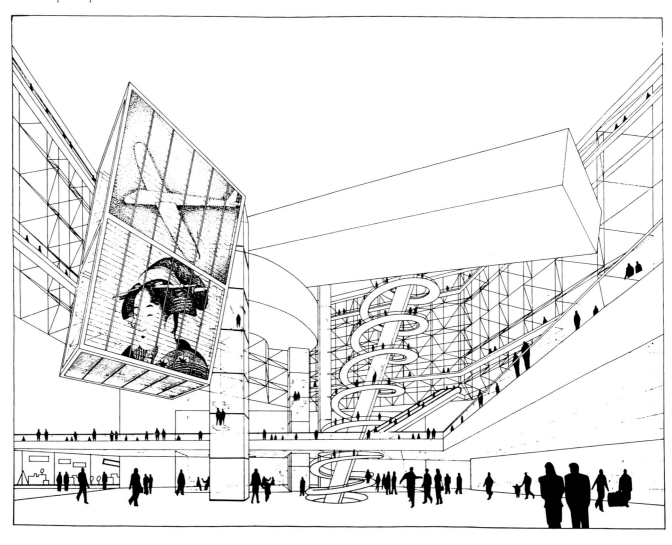

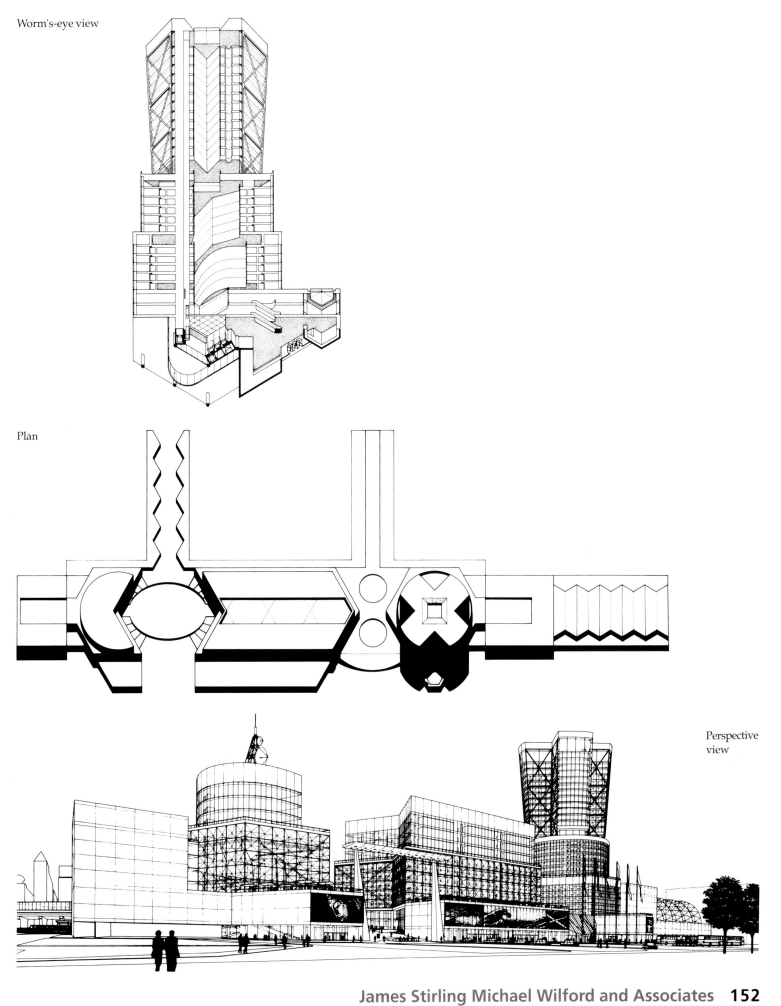

Worm's-eye view

Plan

Perspective
view

The Music School and Theatre Academy, Stuttgart

James Stirling Michael Wilford and Associates

Commissioned *1992*
Building commenced (Music School) *1992*
Completion due *1996*
Client *Land Baden-Württemberg (represented by the Staatliches Hochbauamt I, Stuttgart)*
Quantity Surveyors *Davis Langdon & Everest*
Structural and Services Engineers *Ove Arup and Partners*
Acoustics *Arup Acoustics*
Structural (design development) Engineer *Boll & Partners*
Mechanical Engineer *Jaeger Mornhinweg, Ingenieurbüro Fritz Spieth*
Electrical Engineer *Ingenieurbüro Burrer*
Acoustics *Müller BBM GmbH*

Worm's-eye
axonometric

The Music School and Theatre Academy courtyard
that leads off Konrad-Adenauer-Strasse

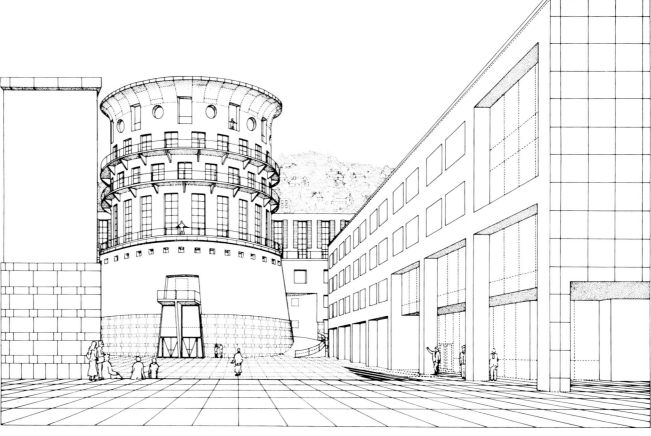

Plans for a new complex for the Music School and Theatre Academy adjoining the new Staatsgalerie complete the sequence of structures and public spaces along the 'cultural mile' flanking Konrad-Adenauer-Strasse. The urban composition continues the principle of three-sided external spaces semi-enclosed by buildings opening towards the city, initiated by the original Staatsgalerie (1837) and continued with the new Staatsgalerie and Theatre Garden (1984).

A lay-by on Konrad-Adenauer-Strasse accommodates taxis and vehicles. Passengers can alight at the foot of a ramp, by which they can reach the public terrace and enter the Theatre Academy from the terrace. The Music School can be entered from the new plaza. The plaza has a reverse perspective and is sloped towards and below the terrace. External surfaces are designed to be similar to those of the new Staatsgalerie and will include veneered sandstone and travertine walls and natural stone paving. Internally, materials will be different, responding to the building's acoustic needs with timber panelling, timber floors, and carpeting. Whereas the main feature of the exterior of the Staatsgalerie is its walls, the exterior of the Music School and Theatre Academy emphasises windows (which are functionally necessary). Those walls on which the random positioning of windows relates to the varied sizes of the rooms have a superimposed grid of stone pilasters to establish a visual order.

The environment of Urbanstrasse and Eugenstrasse will be improved as the façades of the new buildings bring the unequal heights that occur along the street into unison. The long façade on Urbanstrasse will be subdivided (by escape stairs) into smaller dimensions related to the scale of the buildings in the street.

The Stirling-designed Staatsgalerie is to the left of the model. *Photo: Peter Walser*

Bookshop for the Venice Biennale

James Stirling Michael Wilford and Associates

Commission 1989
Constructed 1992
Working Drawings and Construction Management
    G. B. Cuman, M. Del Favero, S. Calcinoni
General Contractor *Daniele Jacorossi SpA*

Site plan

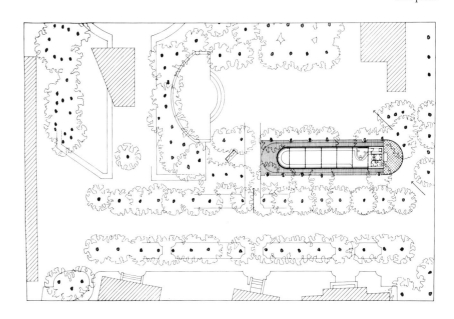

The bookshop sits among the trees of the
Biennale gardens near the Italian pavilion

Elevation

The Biennale site is a large public garden near the Arsenale in Venice. The exhibition buildings representing various countries are freestanding pavilions set among trees. The 'bookship-boatshop' is approximately 200 metres square and is located near the Italian pavilion. It is in a strategic position between the avenues of trees that border the main public footpath leading from the *vaporetto*. The long, single-storey is surmounted by an illuminated rooftop sign denoting the entrance. A laser within the roof drum sends beams of coloured light through the overhanging tree branches and into the sky — markers that are visible from the lagoon.

The sloping roof is sheathed in copper and lined on its underside in redwood boarding. Eaves project over the boardwalk, which runs around the three glazed sides of the bookshop. The roof creates a continuous shaded awning above the shop window, which has a permanent display of the art books and catalogues for sale within. A raised clerestory running along the centre of the building provides daylighting.

Books are laid out flat for browsing along a continuous timber bench top, approximately 40 metres in length. Books are also stored below the bench top in 'honeycomb' shelving units lining the perimeter of the shop. Roof trusses support a central duct that carries the air-conditioning, main lighting, and alarm systems. The plant room is located in the mezzanine over the entrance lobby, and a pair of external shutters allows replacement of machinery directly from the outside by means of a mobile electric hoist.

Temasek Polytechnic, Singapore
James Stirling Michael Wilford and Associates
in association with DP Architects PTE

Commission 1990
Commenced 1993
Completion due 1995
Client Temasek Polytechnic and the Public Works Department

Schematic design:
Structure, mechanical, electrical,
and special services Ove Arup and Partners
Acoustics Arup Acoustics

Design development:
Mechanical & electrical Services Engineer Ewbank Preece
 Engineers plc
Structural Engineer Ove Arup Singapore
Acoustics Acviron

Quantity Surveyor KPK Singapore
Landscape Consultant PDAA Singapore
Contractors Lee Kin Tah / Woh Hup

Temasek Polytechnic will accommodate 11,400 students, an academic staff of 800 – 1,000, with a support staff of 500. It will constitute a city of learning of approximately 13,000 persons. At the centre of the school complex is a public plaza that reflects the polytechnic's open relationship with the Singapore community. The horseshoe-shaped administration building is a focal point of the polytechnic. Elevated on columns, it shelters a promenade that encircles the plaza and houses banks, shops, and exhibition galleries. Beneath the plaza is a 600-seat auditorium and a 250-seat multipurpose theatre.
The four schools — Applied Science, Business, Design, and Technology — have concourse entrances off the promenade. These concourses are sheltered by the upper levels and extended to shade outdoor spaces. The schools are designed to balance vertical and horizontal movement, with the most densely used spaces, such as lecture theatres, situated on or below concourse level. The highest building is the library, on eleven floors, accommodating 2,000 readers. It will be visible on the Singapore skyline.
An integrated architectural and engineering design process is being pursued to achieve environmentally appropriate energy-efficient solutions. Externally, features such as voids and breezeways are created to encourage as much air movement as possible around pedestrian zones. Internally, the organisation of spaces has been studied to establish optimum room dimensions and façade configurations to minimise energy consumption while maximising elements such as daylight at desk height.

Model of the campus. *Photo: John Donat*

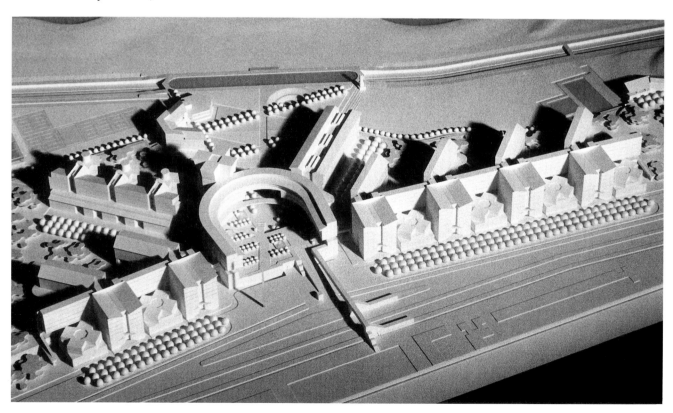

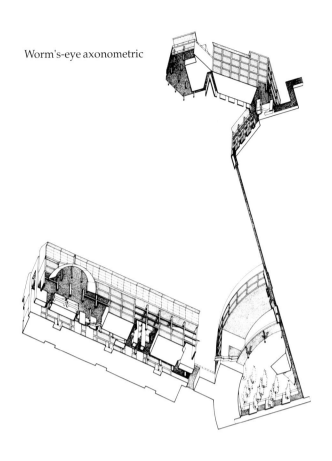

Axonometric of the horseshoe-shaped
administration building positioned around
the public plaza which forms the centre of
the complex. Behind is the library block

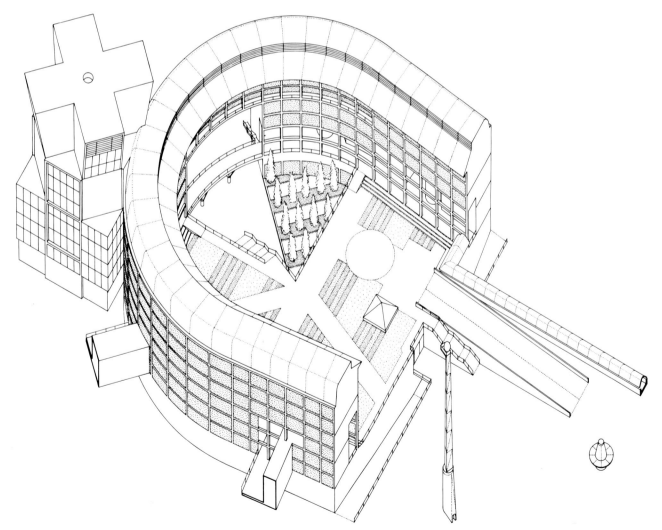

Los Angeles Philharmonic Hall

James Stirling Michael Wilford and Associates

Competition 1988
Client *Disney Hall Committee*
Structural and Services Engineers, Quantity Surveyors
    Ove Arup and Partners
Acoustic Engineers *Arup Acoustics*

View of the lobby interior

Model
Photo: John Donat

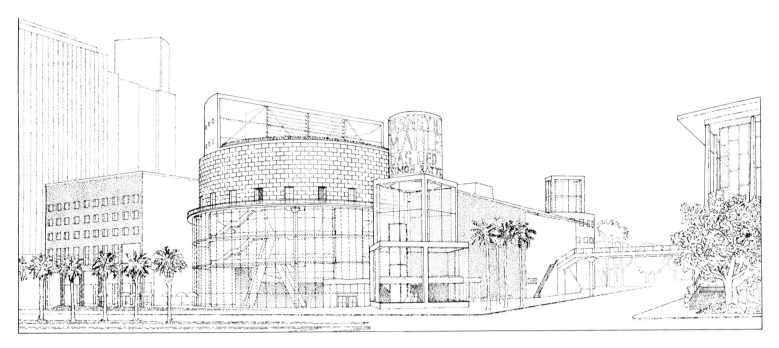

The circular concert hall is the centrepiece of the composition

The design is an ensemble of architectural forms unified at ground level by a grand concourse, a microcosm of the city. The disposition and design of the elements are informal yet geometrically related to the north-south axis of the Los Angeles Music Center.

The circular and stepped concert hall is the centrepiece of the composition. Its diagonal orientation towards the corner of Grand Avenue and First Street reinforces Grand Avenue as the main site of the Music Center. The concert hall, together with the chamber hall and the support facilities building, form a trio of primary elements.

A smaller group of three pavilions containing the gift shop, the box office and the cinema, and the grand staircase and the club lounge are arranged along First Street. These pavilions define the northern entrances to the building and are a visual foil to the large form of the existing Dorothy Chandler Pavilion.

A garden enclosed on three sides by the concert hall, chamber hall, and facilities buildings offers views of downtown and comprises the southern edge of the city block. The upper parts of the buildings semi-enclose a roof terrace with adjoining bars and lounges at the top balcony level of the concert hall. The terrace affords

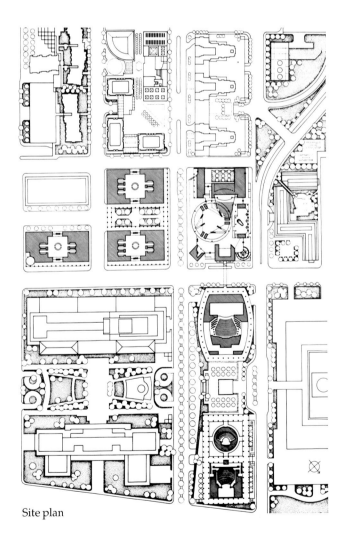

Site plan

View of the Cathedral. *Photo: Nick Carter*

The New Brentwood Cathedral, Essex

Quinlan Terry, Erith and Terry Architects

Commission 1986
Commenced 1989
Completed 1991
Client Brentwood Roman Catholic Diocese Trustees
Main Contractor Sindall Construction Ltd
Structural Engineer I. J. Pennington
Quantity Surveyor Gleeds

The arches and columns form an arcade
that supports the central space. *Photo: Nick Carter*

This building replans a concrete structure from the 1970s that was built as an extension to an existing nineteenth-century Gothic Revival church when the church became a cathedral. The two buildings form an elongated Maltese cross in plan; the old nave becomes the chancel of the new cathedral, with transepts on four sides.

The nave is 43 feet wide by 67 feet long and 36 feet high. The spacing of the columns is dictated by the column shafts that remain on the south side of the church but that were removed in the modern extension. These have been replaced in the new design; thus there are five arches on the north and south sides and three on the east and west. The arches rest on simple Tuscan columns and form an arcade that supports the entire central space. At the corners of this arcade are a pair of giant Doric pilasters with entablature, complete with triglyphs and metopes that encircle the central space. The pilasters also constitute the main architectural element of the building's exterior. In the spandrels of the arcade are roundels containing the Stations of the Cross executed in terracotta by Raphael Maklouf and reminiscent of the Foundling Hospital in Florence by Brunelleschi, which was a major source of inspiration for this design. The proportion of 5 to 3 in the arches is continued above the Doric entablature with patterned grilles and clerestory windows; the space is finished with a fretted and gilded coffered ceiling surrounded by a guilloche pattern. Externally, the giant Doric Order is expressed by pilasters on the north and west. The centre bay of the main entrance on the north elevation forms a portico based on the south portico of Saint Paul's Cathedral and Saint Mary-le-Strand. The walling between the pilasters is of Kentish Rag stone, which matches that of the Gothic Revival church. The building is constructed of solid load-bearing masonry, faced in Kentish Rag stone with reconstructed stone dressing and stucco.

Architecturally, the design of the exterior is a mixture of early Italian Renaissance and the English baroque style practiced by Christopher Wren. The Doric Order is Bramantesque Palladian; the arcade bears the obvious influence of Brunelleschi; and the cupola is inspired by Bernini's church in Ariccia. The windows, however, have characteristically English lead cames fixed to bronze saddle bars with small panes; the clerestory is Smeed Dean brickwork, and the roof is Welsh slate. The juxtaposition of classical and Gothic elements in the west elevation and the view of Gothic arches seen between the columns of a classical arcade is inevitable in any building with such a long history and is common to many English cathedrals.

All five Orders have been employed in the new design: Tuscan for the arcade, Doric for the main giant Order, Ionic for the east and west Serlian windows, and Composite and Corinthian for the organ and cathedra.

opposite: Quinlan Terry's presentation drawing

The new
BRENTWOOD CATHEDRAL

Long Section

East Front

Plan

Front & Side of Cathedra

New Organ Case

North Front

The Gothick Villa, Regent's Park, London
Quinlan Terry, Erith and Terry Architects

Commission 1986
Commenced 1989
Completed 1991
Client *The Crown Estate Commissioners*
Main Contractor *Sindall Construction Ltd*
Structural Engineer *Morton Partnership*
Quantity Surveyor *Gleeds*

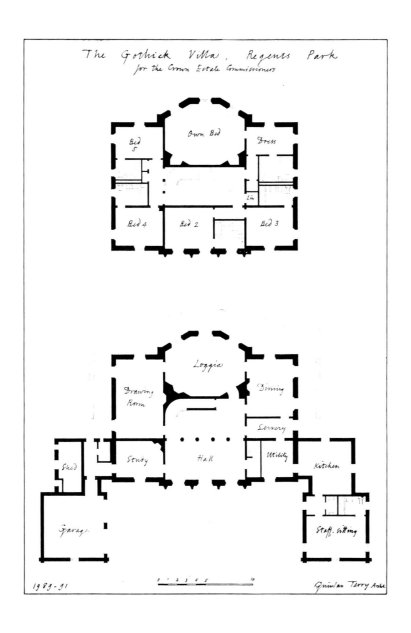

The Gothick Villa is the third of six villas to be built in Regent's Park, London, for the Crown Estate. It was the wish of the client that these new villas should continue the Picturesque tradition established by John Nash in the early nineteenth century. The plan was based originally on Palladio's design for the Villa Sarraceno in the mid-sixteenth century and was conceived as a Tuscan villa with a castellated pediment and cornice. It was then felt that the design should reflect Nash's preoccupation with Gothic style. The final design provides for a pedimented and castellated facade with Gothic Orders reminiscent of Gibbs's Temple of Liberty at Stowe, which uses Batty Langley's Gothic Orders. The front door leads into a large hall featuring marble columns with Corinthian capitals. A marble floor takes its inspiration from a mosque in Cairo. The halls in turn lead to an octagonal loggia with Gothic-style windows and fireplace and a vaulted ceiling influenced by the architecture of John Soane. The basis for much of the detailed work is Nash's Longner Hall, and Combermere Abbey in Shropshire, one of the foremost Gothic Revival buildings done in the Strawberry Hill style. The detailing of the label mouldings, window and door jambs, and door plinths is influenced by a number of medieval East Anglian churches, particularly in Dedham and Higham. The balustrade to the terrace is influenced by the Palazzo Contarini-Fasan, which represents the Venetian precedent of a classical plan with a Gothic-style treatment that was the main theme of the villa's design. The ceiling, the dome, and the pendentives to the staircase hall have their obvious counterparts in the fulsome, almost baroque, elements found in Spanish Gothic cathedrals.

Plans

The front entrance to the Gothick Villa. *Photo: Nick Carter*

Kobe Institute, Saint Catherine's College University of Oxford, Kobe, Japan

Troughton McAslan

Commissioned 1990
Commenced 1990
Completed 1991
Client *Kobe Steel and St Catherine's College, University of Oyford*
Design Team *John McAslan, Piers Smerin, Kevin Lloyd,*
Yasser El Gabry, Murray Smith
Contractor *Takenaka*
Engineer *Ove Arup and Partners*

The Kobe Institute, a branch of Saint Catherine's College at Oxford University, reflects the meeting of two powerful cultural entities: Japanese industry and the European university. This duality is reflected in the project's design. The brief called for a traditional Oxford college in miniature, including housing for students and tutors, classrooms, administration space, a library, a dining hall, and a common room. The site, however, could hardly be more different from the English university town.
Perched on a steep wooded hillside on Rokko Mountain, the institute commands an impressive view of the city of Kobe and Osaka Bay beyond.
Offering one-year courses taught in English, the Kobe Institute is the first such venture by an Oxford college outside the city of Oxford. Troughton McAslan's task was to reinterpret the essential qualities of the college in response to the wholly new setting. For this the architects drew on the building features of Saint Catherine's College, which, built in 1963 by Arne Jacobsen on a semi-rural site, is itself atypical of its context. The design responds to the narrow site with a linear, rhythmic quality that is reminiscent of Jacobsen. It also draws more directly on the architecture of traditional colleges. Like

these, the Institute is centred around a quadrangle formed by the remodelled existing building to the north; the newly built lecture theatre; and a row of new concrete-framed and stone-clad buildings to the south containing student and tutors' housing.

above: The Institute is on a steep wooded site.
Photo: Hiroyuki Hirai

The building reinterprets the essential qualities of the Oxford college
Photo: Hiroyuki Hirai

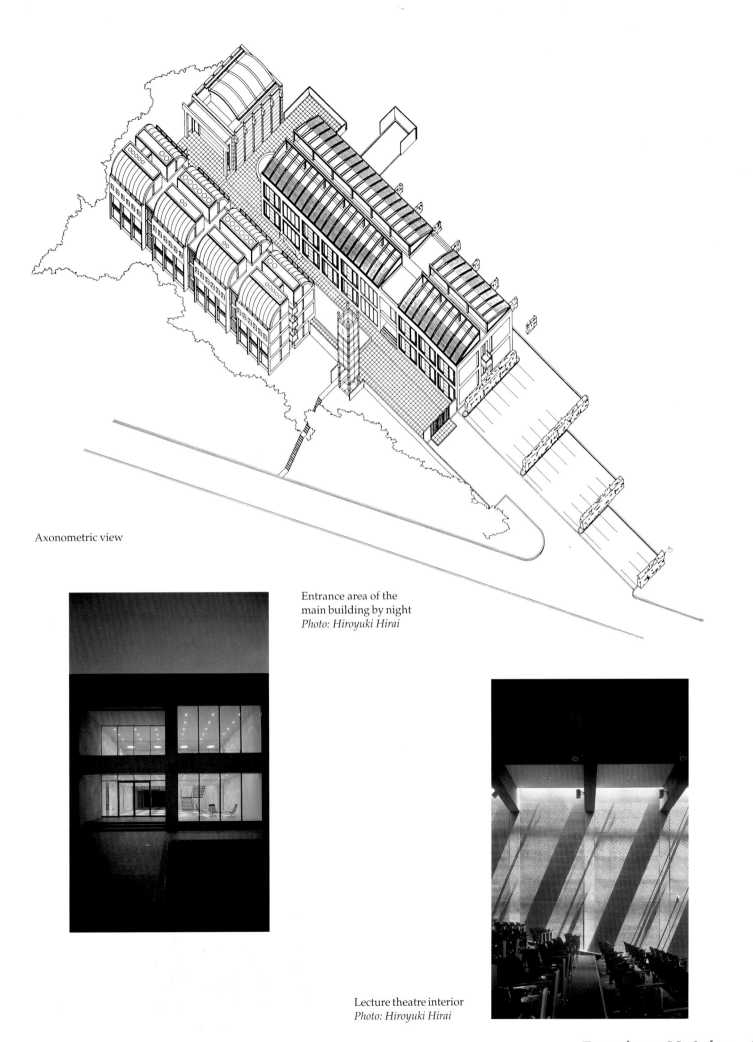

Axonometric view

Entrance area of the
main building by night
Photo: Hiroyuki Hirai

Lecture theatre interior
Photo: Hiroyuki Hirai

Axonometric

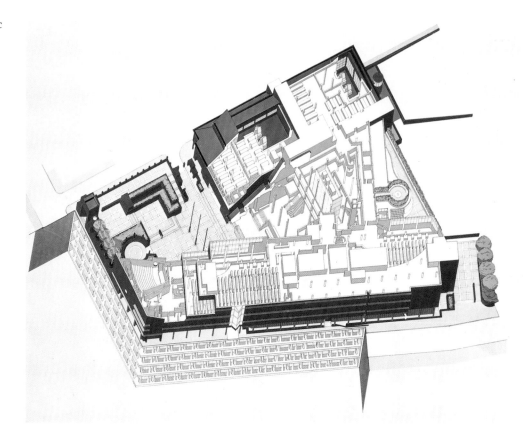

The British Library, St Pancras, London

Colin St John Wilson and Partners

*Leslie Martin and Colin St John Wilson **commissioned***
to design Library for the British Museum, Bloomsbury 1962
*Colin St John Wilson **commissioned** to design British*
Library building, Bloomsbury, to expanded brief 1972
***Feasibility study** for revised site at St Pancras 1975*
***Building commenced** 1983*
***Occupancy planned** in three phases with sub-stages*
***Client** The British Library (user); The Department*
of National Heritage (sponsor)
***Main Contractors** Laing Management*
(first phase management contractor);
Sir Robert McAlpine / Haden Young
(second phase, joint venture contractor)
***Structural Engineers** Ove Arup and Partners*
***Services Engineer** Steensen Varming & Mulcahy*

Sectional model through
entrance hall.
Photo: John Donat

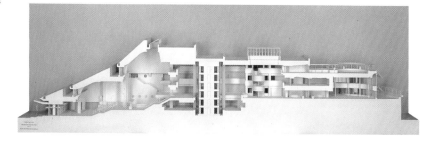

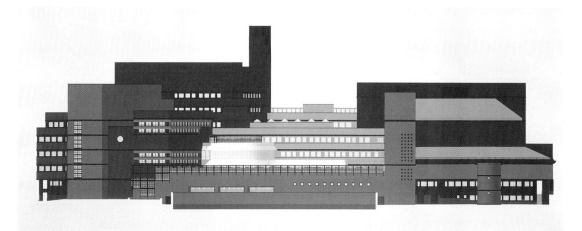

Silkscreen print
of the north
elevation

The closed access Humanities Reading Room. Oil on canvas by Carl Laubin

View of the entrance hall. *Photo: John Donat*

The new British Library is arguably the grandest contemporary public building project in Britain of its time. Set next to George Gilbert Scott's extravagant Victorian Midland Hotel, which fronts St Pancras Station, the imposing red brick building owes more to Alvar Aalto than to Scott. The building replaces the existing British Library, which currently forms part of the British Museum complex in Bloomsbury.

The library houses the national collection of books, manuscripts, maps, and patents as well as exhibition galleries, conservation laboratories, offices, and lecture rooms. The building provides for two very different main patterns of use: The humanities section features closed-access reading rooms in which readers are supplied with books from the storage basement; the science and patent section contains an open-access collection, and readers are able to find publications, abstracts, and microfiches for themselves. Between these two sections lies the main entrance hall from which access to the public areas is obtained. The hall is a grand space, rising to the full height of the building. The hall is entered from an enclosed courtyard screened from the traffic of Euston Road. The courtyard is divided by steps, ramps, and large-scale plantings into separate areas, one of which is a small, circular amphitheatre. The building was designed for expansion in three phases of which only one is now being constructed.

The Checkpoint Charlie building by OMA, 1989. Oil on canvas

Checkpoint Charlie
Zoe Zenghelis

Painting of a project in Berlin by OMA
(Office for Metropolitan Architecture) 1989

Political change has been responsible for a dramatic shift in the circumstances surrounding Checkpoint Charlie. The result of a collaboration between the military and the municipality of Kreuzberg, the building by OMA intentionally echoes the forms of the Berlin Wall and the viewing towers that were once so close to it. The ground floor was planned as a service facility for Allied troops and the upper levels were given over to apartments of various sizes. A distinct podium base, which separated these two functions, was intended to make the division between them clear. Direct metaphors such as the roof, which is clad in polished metal and seems to fly over the building like an aeroplane wing, continue this formal theme and make an unmistakeable reference to specific events in the history of the city.

Although the Berlin Wall has now been removed, this particular piece of real estate still evokes strong mental images of the divided city. The painting of the Checkpoint Charlie project by Zoe Zenghelis has captured the essence of these images, with a cool grey and white palette used to convey the complicated texture of the memories associated with this gateway through the wall. While other paintings by Zenghelis have also featured architecture as the focal point of a depopulated world, the empty, lifeless street that is shown here effectively communicates a silence of another sort.

z.zenghelis

Architects' biographies

List of abbreviations used

CBE   Commander of the Order of the
British Empire
RA   Royal Academician
RIBA   Royal Institute of British Architects

Robert Adam (b. 1948) trained at the Polytechnic of Central London and was awarded a Rome Scholarship in 1973. His practice is part of the long-established firm of Winchester Design (Architects) Ltd, but is identified primarily with Adam's own built work, predominantly a free and varied expression of the classical tradition, which has been exhibited throughout the world. Adam has written and lectured on various aspects of architectural theory, and in 1989 Viking/Penguin published *Classical Architecture: A Complete Handbook*, his standard work on the subject. Major current projects include a building in Paternoster Square, London; houses for the Duchy of Cornwall; a visitors' centre at Nymans Gardens for the National Trust; additions to the rear of the Ashmolean Museum, Oxford; and an extension to Rhodes House, Oxford.

Allies and Morrison Architects was founded in 1984 by Bob Allies (b. 1953) and Graham Morrison (b. 1951). Allies trained at Edinburgh University, after which he worked for various architects, including Michael Glickman and Michael Brawne. A Rome Scholar in Architecture in 1981–82, he lectured at Cambridge University from 1983 to 1987. Morrison trained at Cambridge University and worked for Keijo Petaja in Finland, and for architects in England including the firm YRM Architects. He was elected national member of the Council of the RIBA in 1991 and was Chairman of the RIBA's Exhibitions Committee from 1992 to 1993. Partner Ian Sutherland (b. 1960) trained in engineering and architecture at Cambridge University, and his

drawings have been widely exhibited and published. Following the practice's early success in the open competition for a new public square at The Mound, Edinburgh, it has been involved with many sites and buildings of historical significance, including the Manor Farm housing development in Kent, and the Clove Building, Butler's Wharf, and 3-4 Ashland Place, as well as new premises for Scott Howard and the Stephen Bull restaurant, all projects in London. Projects in progress include the refurbishment of London's Centre Point (and the creation of a new public square on the site) and London House in the City; the new British Embassy in Dublin; Liverpool's Pierhead civic scheme; Blandford Street (housing/retail units), and an office building in Whitechapel High Street, both in London; Sarum Hall School, London; and the Essex University Library extension. In 1993 the practice won a commission to redesign the interior of the Royal Festival Hall on London's South Bank.

Armstrong Architects was formed in 1986 by Kenneth Armstrong (b. 1954) following the dissolution the previous year of Armstrong Chipperfield, his practice with architect David Chipperfield. He trained at the Mackintosh School of Art in Glasgow and at the Royal College of Art, and went on to work for Foster Associates on the Hong Kong and Shanghai Banking Corporation headquarters. Jenifer Armstrong (b. 1961) joined the practice after training at the Bartlett School of Architecture and Planning, University College, London, and became a partner in 1989. Armstrong Architects operates from offices in Paris and London. The U.K. projects include the Imperial War Museum shop in London; headquarters for Elementer Industrial Design in Slough and London; offices and showrooms in Frankfurt and London for Voko (U.K.); offices for the pop group U2; and private residences in London. The architects

have carried out major masterplanning studies for Tarmac Properties and MEPC and have acted as design consultants to Sir Norman Foster and Partners on the proposed urban regeneration programme for King's Cross, London. Winning competition entries include the design for the Maison de la Culture du Japon in Paris, due for completion in 1996; and the practice was placed second in a competition for new headquarters for the Banco de Portugal. Their work has been exhibited in London and Paris, and current projects include preliminary designs for a hotel in Knightsbridge.

Arup Associates was established in 1963 by the engineer Ove Arup (1895–1988) and the architect Philip Dowson (b. 1924), as a parallel partnership to Ove Arup and Partners, an internationally known engineering practice begun in the U.K. in 1949. Over the years, the firm of architects, engineers, and quantity surveyors has also become a global concern, pioneering the employment of established multi-disciplinary teams as part of the design process. Its work over the past two decades has covered masterplanning (such as the regeneration of Stockley Park near Heathrow Airport into a thriving business park); industrial and commercial development; office buildings (such as IBM U.K., near Portsmouth, and 1 Finsbury Avenue, an office, retail, and leisure development in London); university residential and faculty buildings (at Oxford and Cambridge universities); schools; the rehabilitation of old buildings (including the Maltings Concert Hall at Snape in East Anglia); sports and leisure facilities (such as the International Garden Festival Hall in Liverpool, the Sussex Stand at Goodwood Racecourse, and the Diplomatic Corps Sports Club for Riyadh); theatres; concert halls; and museums. Much of the practice's work has been won in competitions, including, most recently, the International Concert Hall and Cultural Centre in Istanbul. Many projects have won both RIBA and Civic Trust Awards, including phases one to four of Broadgate in the City of London. In 1990 the Imperial War Museum project received *The Sunday Times*/Royal Fine Art Commission Building of the Year Award. Sir Philip Dowson CBE was from 1969 to 1990 a partner in Ove Arup and Partners and is now a consultant to the practice. In 1979 he was elected a Royal Academician. He was knighted for his services to architecture in 1980, and in 1981 he received the Royal Gold Medal. In December 1993 he was elected President of the Royal Academy of Arts.

Birds Portchmouth Russum Architects is a London-based practice. Andrew Birds (b. 1960) trained at Leeds Polytechnic and the Polytechnic of Central London. Richard Portchmouth and Michael Russum (both born in 1956) trained at Kingston Polytechnic. The three architects were engaged by James Stirling Michael Wilford and Associates during the 1980s, working on projects such as the Bilbao transport interchange and a mixed commercial development in Seville. In 1988 they won a RIBA competition to design the Avenue de Chartres car park in Chichester and established their practice the following year. The £ 6m was completed in 1991 and received several awards, including ones from RIBA and the Civic Trust. Among the subsequent competition projects are the Stonehenge Visitors' Centre; the seafront at Morecambe in Lancashire; the Royal Museum of Scotland; housing in Haarlem in the Netherlands; a railway station for Crossrail in Rickmansworth; and Moulsecoombe Health Clinic. The work of the practice has been shown in various exhibitions, and the partners have lectured at RIBA and at educational institutions in Germany and the USA.

Building Design Partnership, known as BDP, was formed in 1961 as an integrated practice of architects, engineers, and surveyors and now maintains offices throughout the U.K. and in Paris and Berlin. Major projects have included the British Channel Tunnel Terminal at Folkestone; London's Crossrail project; headquarters for the Halifax Building Society; the J.P. Morgan and the Adam Opel AG headquarters in Rüsselsheim, Germany; and retail developments such as the Ealing

Centre, Bentall Centre, Kingston on Thames, and Whiteleys of Bayswater, all in London. Richard Saxon (b. 1942), chairman of BDP's London office, worked on the award-winning Halifax Building Society headquarters, the Milburngate Centre in Durham, and the Merseyside Maritime Museum masterplan in Liverpool. He was design partner for the masterplan of the All England Lawn Tennis and Croquet Club at Wimbledon, and has published books on the design and development of atrium buildings. Richard Rees (b. 1955), who executed the drawings for the Wimbledon project, is an associate architect of BDP. His international experience in large-scale sports projects and leisure projects stems from nine years spent working in Hong Kong as an urban designer, architect, and illustrator on such projects as the Stadium Grandstand Project for the Royal Hong Kong Jockey Club.

Cecil Denny Highton is a leading architectural and conservation practice, with offices in London, Warsaw, and Gibraltar that has received many awards, including the Europa Nostra Medal of Honour for its conservation work at the Foreign and Commonwealth Office. During the last fifteen years it has completed work on some of the most important historic buildings in London, among them the Foreign and Commonwealth Offices, the Natural History Museum, the Old War Office and Admiralty Building in Whitehall, the Victoria and Albert Museum, and the Home Office. John Denny (b. 1941) became Senior Partner in Raymond J. Cecil's practice in 1990, on Cecil's retirement, and introduced to the firm his interest in the conservation of historic buildings, which dates back to the early 1960s. The group's areas of expertise now also include the estate of the Royal Household, government buildings, corporate headquarters, and museums. In 1992–93, in association with Kenzo Tange and Howard, Needles, Tammen, and Bergendoff, the practice created the master plan and design for the stadium in the main sports complex for the Manchester 2000 Olympics bid.

Chapman Taylor Partners was formed in 1959 and is a leading practice made up of architects and town planners based in London. Well known for its office buildings, the firm designs housing, industrial projects, business

parks and shopping centres and undertakes conservation projects. The New Scotland headquarters in Victoria Street, London, for the Metropolitan Police, completed in 1966, was the forerunner of a series of major office buildings, such as the Rank Hovis McDougall Tower, the twin towers of King's Cross House, and One Drummond Gate. In recent years new offices in the City of London, Westminster, and Mayfair have been built, including Friary Court for Commercial Union, and Lansdowne House for Legal & General Assurance Society. Outside London, the project to design the headquarters for Pearl Assurance, Peterborough, included furniture and fittings.

Robert Chitham (b. 1934), a partner at Chapman Taylor Partners since 1988, is responsible for the practice's conservation work and historic settings development, including proposed new developments at Dorchester, Cirencester, and Chichester, and rehabilitation work off Park Lane in central London and in Covent Garden. The firm currently maintains offices in London, Paris, Leipzig, Cologne, Brussels, and Sydney and has an increasing involvement with new retail and office projects in the U.K. and internationally, including London Bridge City (an office development), a City Challenge project in Brixton based on the South London transport interchange, masterplanning studies for the Wien Mitte station in Vienna, and the La Seyne docks in Toulon.

Simon Conder trained and qualified in London both as an architect at the Architectural Association and as an industrial designer at the Royal College of Art. Before starting his own practice, he worked for firms in London and Copenhagen, most recently as an architect in the public sector where he completed major housing schemes in Basildon New Town and the London Borough of Lambeth. He formed his own firm, **Simon Conder Associates** in 1984, working first on conversion and residential projects, but also for the London Docklands Corporation on studies for dock use. Since 1986 the range of his work has broadened to include new-build projects on urban and rural sites, interior design, and retail shop, exhibition, and product design. Much of his work has been awarded in competitions, and since 1988 the practice has also been designing outside the U.K., in Germany, Japan, and Hawaii. Commercial clients include English Estates (rural workshops in Suffolk), First Leisure Corporation, Next, and Sealink Ferries.

Peter Cook is currently Professor and Head of Architecture at the Bartlett School of Architecture and Planning, University College, London. In 1984 he was appointed Head of the Department of Architecture and Professor of Architecture at the Städelschule in Frankfurt, Germany. In 1986 he was elected Pro Rector, and in 1988 he was appointed Life Professor. He was born in 1936 and studied at the Architectural Association from 1958 to 1960. In 1964 he began teaching at the Architectural Association and has taught there ever since. He has been in practice in London with Christine Hawley since 1976. In 1961 Cook was one of the instigators of Archigram, a loosely formed group of architects based in London that became formalised in 1968 and continued to work on collaborative projects until 1976. The group published eight magazines between 1961 and 1970. Archigram subscribed to 'architecture by drawing' as a method, embracing pop culture and new technology, and reinventing the formal nature of the city. The group's most striking utopian projects include the Plug-In City (1964), Control and Choice (shown at the Paris Biennale in 1967), Instant City (1968), and Urban Mark (1972). Archigram's work was presented in a touring exhibition organised by the Kunsthalle in Vienna in 1994. Cook's own projects include Arcadia City (1976–78) and Real City, Frankfurt (1984). Cook and Hawley's joint projects include Roosevelt Island Housing (with Ron Herron and others); the Langen Glass Museum; the Städel Museum extension, Frankfurt; the Hamburg riverside (with Ron Herron); housing at Lützowplatz, Berlin (for IBA, 1989); the Pavilion for Expo '90, Osaka; a canteen block for the Städelschule, Frankfurt; and experimental housing/workshops for mature residents in Edinburgh. In 1991 Cook's *New Spirit in Architecture,* with Rosie Llewelyn-Jones, was published.

Julian Cowie (b. 1965) trained as an architect at the University of Newcastle upon Tyne and at the Royal College of Art. His tutor at the college was the architect James Gowan, and Cowie subsequently worked with him on the Ospedale Nuovo project in Milan. He

has since worked for Denton Scott and Allies and Morrison and has pursued his own work through commissions and competitions. In 1991 Cowie won the Royal Academy Award for Architecture (student prize).

Edward Cullinan Architects was established in 1959 by Edward Cullinan CBE (b. 1930). Cullinan trained as an architect at Cambridge University and at the Architectural Association and then took up a fellowship at the University of California before working with Sir Denys Lasdun. He has taught architecture, both in the U.K. and in the USA, throughout his career. The practice is organised as a cooperative and has completed projects ranging from £5,000 to £19m. The firm's work has won many RIBA and Civic Trust awards. Among the winning buildings are the Minster Lovell Mill Conference Centre; the Parish Church of Saint Mary Barnes; Lambeth Community Care Centre; and headquarters for the R.M.C. group plc, Thorpe, Surrey. In 1990 the practice won the Europa Nostra Medal of Honour for its Fountains Abbey Visitor Centre in Yorkshire. Current projects include a new library at Saint John's College, Cambridge University; a new media centre in Cheltenham; Bristol University Sports and Recreation Centre; the Stonehenge Visitor Centre; and a new International Manufacturing Centre at the University of Warwick. Edward Cullinan was elected a Royal Academician in 1989.

Jeremy Dixon.Edward Jones first worked together on their successful competition entry in 1972 for the design of offices for Northamptonshire County Council. Both trained at the Architectural Association, graduating in 1963. Dixon (b. 1930) built a number of housing projects in London, mainly in Westminster, and went on to design the restaurant at the Tate Gallery. In 1983, his limited competition design, in association with Building Design Partnership, for the Royal Opera House, Covent Garden, was selected, and he was one of six architects invited to submit schemes for the Sainsbury Wing of the National Gallery. While in independent practice, Jones (b. 1939) won first prize in an international competition for Mississauga City Hall in Canada, and his design won the Governor General's Award in 1990. The two architects set up in partnership together as Jeremy Dixon.Edward Jones in 1989, working on commissions for the Royal Opera House,

the Henry Moore Foundation, Darwin College in Cambridge, the University of Portsmouth, the Robert Gordon University in Aberdeen, the Cardiff Bay Development Corporation, and J. Sainsbury plc. At the 1991 Venice Biennale, 'A Gateway to Venice', the firm's entry for an open international competition, won first prize and has been subsequently exhibited in London and Venice. The new galleries for the Henry Moore Institute in Leeds, designed by the practice with Building Design Partnership, opened in 1993. The architects are currently designing an urban regeneration scheme in the centre of Bradford, Yorkshire. Dixon has taught at the Architectural Association and the Royal College of Art and has lectured widely. Jones was senior tutor at the Royal College of Art from 1975 to 1982, and he has taught at various American universities. His book, *Guide to the Architecture of London*, written with Christopher Woodward, was published in 1983, with a revised edition appearing in 1992.

Evans and Shalev have been in practice as architects and planning consultants since 1965. Eldred Evans qualified at the Architectural Association in 1961; David Shalev trained at the Technion School of Architecture in Israel, qualifying in 1960. Both have a long-standing involvement with the academic world, as teachers and as external examiners, at a number of colleges in the U.K. and on RIBA boards. Their portfolio has been a diverse one, with projects completed in Vienna, Jerusalem, the Bahamas, and Australia, as well as throughout the U.K. In 1988 the practice completed an award-winning three-year project for Truro Crown Courts, the regional Courts of Justice in Cornwall, and completed Meopham 2000, a rural masterplan in Kent. Recent projects include the Ocean Village in St Austell, Cornwall; The Centrum, an office redevelopment in London; and the Tate Gallery St Ives in Cornwall. The practice is currently working on the Bede Museum at Jarrow, and on a new building for Jesus College at Cambridge University, both the result of premediated competitions.

Feary + Heron Architects is a London-based practice formed in 1984 by Julian Feary and Katharine Heron, both of whom trained at the Architectural Association. Projects completed prior to this date include the conversion of buildings into an art gallery for the artist Ian Hamilton Finlay; the reconstruction of Paul Nash's design for a bathroom for Tilly Losch for the exhibition *The Thirties* at the Hayward Gallery; and the conversion of pier buildings on Orkney into the Piers Art Centre, which won both a Civic Trust Award and a recent Museum of the Year Award. The practice has worked extensively for artists and art collectors and has completed restoration schemes for stone buildings in Cornwall and Yorkshire. Recent projects include the Mudchute Park and Farm on the Isle of Dogs; the restoration of housing in Clerkenwell and Spitalfields in East London; a crafts advisory service room for Oriel Gallery in Cardiff, Wales; the design and installation of features such as decorative windows for the Tate Gallery St Ives in Cornwall; banners for the Chelsea and Westminster Hospital in London; and, most recently, the extension and renovation of existing spaces at the Camden Arts Centre.

Sir Norman Foster and Partners was first established as Foster Associates in 1967 by Norman and Wendy Foster (and was subsequently renamed in 1992). Now an internationally renowned practice employing a staff of over 250 worldwide, with offices in London, Berlin, Frankfurt, Hong Kong, Nîmes, and Tokyo, its work has received over eighty awards and citations. In 1993 Sir Norman Foster, who has been a Royal Academician since his election in 1983, received a Gold Medal from the AIA. Foster was born in Manchester in 1935 and trained at the university there before continuing his studies on a Henry Fellowship at Yale University. In 1963 he founded Team 4 in collaboration with his wife Wendy and with Richard and Su Rogers. Early successes included the Willis Faber & Dumas head office in Ipswich (1971–75, now a listed building) and the Renault Centre in Swindon (1984). Many of his practice's projects have resulted from international competitions, including the Sainsbury Centre for the Visual Arts at the University of East Anglia (1978); the Hong Kong and Shanghai Banking Corporation headquarters (1979–86); the Torres de Coliserola, a communications tower in Barcelona (1988–92), and the Bilbao Metro (1988); Stansted Airport in Essex (1981–91); Century Tower in Tokyo (1987–91); the Carré d'Art, a cultural centre in Nîmes (1984–93); and a li-

brary for the Cranfield Institute of Technology (1989–92). The Sackler Galleries project for the Royal Academy of Arts (1985–91) was named RIBA Building of the Year in 1993. The practice has designed masterplans for sites at King's Cross in London; Nîmes and Cannes in France; Berlin and Duisburg in Germany; and Rotterdam in Holland. Shops have also been designed for Esprit and Katherine Hamnett, and furniture for Tecno. In 1993 the practice won the competition to redesign the Reichstag, to house the new German Parliament in Berlin. Foster is currently working on a new airport for Hong Kong at Chek Lap Kok and many other projects, including the Musée de la Préhistoire in the Gorges du Verdon in France; a masterplan for the Lisbon Expo; new headquarters for the Commerzbank in Frankfurt; a viaduct in Rennes, France; and an extension to the Joslyn Art Museum in Omaha, Nebraska.

Future Systems was founded in 1979 by Jan Kiplicky (b. 1937 in Prague) and David Nixon (b. 1947), and the London office is now headed by Kaplicky and Amanda Levete (b. 1955). Both architects had worked previously for a number of other firms. Kaplicky initially practiced on his own, and then for Sir Denys Lasdun, Piano + Rogers, Louis de Soissons, and Foster Associates. Levete worked for Alsop & Lyall, YRM Architects, as half of Powis & Levete, and for Richard Rogers Partnership. Future Systems' technologically creative designs utilise space-industry construction techniques and environmentally friendly materials, but as yet relatively few of their hundreds of designs have been put into production. Projects at a variety of scales include an energy-efficient kindergarten; the conversion of Thames river barges into accommodation for the homeless; a space station boardroom table for NASA; a spire commemorating the year 2000, with observation platforms, bars, and restaurants; a double-skin 'astrodome' building; a peanut-shaped wilderness retreat; a tower for the Atlanta 1996 Olympics; a natural disaster shelter; and temporary exhibition structures. Recent designs include those for a number of private houses in London and Hertfordshire; a limited-competition entry for a Visitor Centre at Stonehenge; a technology park in Brno, Czech Republic (in association with Richard Rogers Partnership); an aero-

dynamically shaped, energy-efficient office complex for a competition held by the Department of the Environment in Hamburg; and 'The Green Building', an extensive research project carried out by Ove Arup and Partners, a radical examination of the twentieth-century office building. The work of the practice has been widely published throughout the world, and both partners regularly undertake lecture tours abroad.

Nicholas Grimshaw & Partners was established in 1980 by Nicholas Grimshaw (b. 1939), who is Chairman of the practice. He was made Commander of the Order of the British Empire (CBE) in 1993. He trained at the Architectural Association and worked in private practice from 1965 to 1980. In the 1970s Grimshaw became known for his industrial buildings in England for international companies, such as Citroën, Zanussi, Herman Miller, and BMW. The assembly plant for Herman Miller in Bath won a number of awards. The practice has since widened the scope of its work to include sports and leisure complexes, commercial and retail buildings, and projects for the media, such as the award-winning printing works in London's Docklands for the *Financial Times* newspaper. Recent major public commissions include the British Pavilion at Expo 92 in Seville, the Waterloo International Terminal in London, and the *Western Morning News* headquarters and press building in Plymouth, England. Grimshaw has lectured internationally and judged many major competitions throughout the world. The work of his practice was recently showcased in the RIBA exhibition *Structure, Space and Skin* (1993).

Philip Gumuchdjian is a London-based architect who has worked for Richard Rogers Partnership since 1980. Born in 1958, he trained at the Architectural Association and at the Royal College of Art. He has contributed to many of Rogers' projects, including the Coin Street development, the National Gallery competition, 'London as it could be' proposals, the Royal Albert Docks development, the Nice masterplan, the Vienna Twin Towers competition, and proposals for the South Kensington Museums Millenium project. He was responsible for the installation of the exhibition *The New Architecture: Foster, Rogers and Stirling* at the Royal Academy of Arts in 1986 and the Richard Rogers exhibition at the Venice Biennale in 1992. He collaborated on Richard Rogers and Mark Fisher's *A New London* (Penguin, 1993). His own scheme for 'Albertopolis 2025' was exhibited in the Royal Academy Summer Exhibition in 1992.

Hampshire County Architect's Department, led by County Architect Sir Colin Stansfield Smith (b. 1923), is widely renowned for the high standards of its work in the public sector within the county of Hampshire in England. Its reputation was confirmed in 1991 when Sir Colin Stansfield Smith was awarded the RIBA Gold Medal. He joined the Department in 1974 and since that date has been instrumental in changing attitudes towards building design within local government, improving the standards of school buildings in particular. The Department has won numerous other awards from RIBA, and from the Civic Trust, for educational buildings in the county, including Fort Hill Secondary School in Basingstoke; Crestwood Secondary School in Eastleigh; Farnborough College of Technology; Velmead Infant School in Fleet; and Newlands Primary School in Yateley. The County Architect's Department's design for its own premises also received many awards, particularly for energy efficiency. The Department has also commissioned many architectural firms to design projects within the county, including Ahrends Burton Koralek, MacCormac Jamieson Prichard, and Plinke Leaman and Browning. Stephen Clow (b. 1963) and David Morriss (b. 1959) led a team that developed the Department's design for the Hampshire Record Office in Winchester, and David Morriss collaborated with Bob Wallbridge and Tina Bird on the design of the Southampton Magistrates Courthouse complex. Clow trained at the University of Glasgow and joined the Department in 1987. Morriss trained at Portsmouth Polytechnic and joined the department in 1983. Architectural projects that he has been associated with have been shown in the Royal Academy Summer Exhibition on a number of occasions.

Nicholas Hare Architects was formed in 1977. Since then, the practice has grown to its present size, with about fifteen employees; a sole principal, Nicholas Hare; and two associates, Jeremy Bailey and Carol Lelliott. Hare was born in 1942 and studied architecture at Liverpool University and University College in London. Before starting Nicholas Hare Architects, he worked for Arup Associates for eight years, sharing responsibility for many award-winning buildings. From 1977 to 1987 he lectured in architecture at Cambridge University. Jeremy Bailey was born in 1957 and studied architecture at Jesus College, Cambridge University. He joined the practice in 1985. Carol Lelliott was born in 1958 and studied architecture at Girton College at Cambridge University. She joined the practice in 1983, and both associates have been visiting lecturers in architecture at University College in London. The practice's recent university buildings include the Islamic Arts Centre for the School of Oriental and African Studies at the University of London, a £6 million project due for completion in 1995; the Learning Resources Centre at Wye College at the University of London; student housing at the University of Essex; and Bene't Court at Corpus Christi College at Cambridge University. The firm's buildings for industry and commerce include the Business Development Centre at Milton Park, Abingdon; the masterplan for a twenty-two-acre business park in Loughborough for British Gas; and a project for Grosvenor Waterside at Cardiff Bay.

Harper Mackay is a London-based practice with two directors, David Harper (b. 1956) and Ken Mackay (b. 1959). Harper (who trained at the Mackintosh School of Architecture in Glasgow) was in charge of one arm of Nicholas Grimshaw's office while the practice was working on J. Sainsbury's Camden Town supermarket branch in London, the Waterloo International Terminal in London, and the British Pavilion for Expo '92 in Seville, executing thirty-two projects during his tenure. Ken Mackay (who trained at the Canterbury School of Architecture and at the Royal College of Art) worked with Jeremy Dixon on his winning competition design for the extension to the Royal Opera House in Covent Garden and was subsequently invited to develop proposals to extend the National Gallery. The firm's work is wide-ranging, encompassing projects for commercial, industrial, cultural, leisure, retail, sports, educational, and medical facilities. In 1993 Harper Mackay completed London offices for Sony U.K. and Sony Europe; Virgin Radio; and Banks Partnership, one of a number of advertising agency clients. In 1992 the practice undertook a £2 million office design project for Lintas at Canary Wharf, and it is currently working on Heron Quays in London Docklands, a 1.5 million-square-foot office development on a site that includes the Docklands Museum and a public observation deck. This project is one of five projects for Tarmac Brookglade Properties plc, due to be completed in London Docklands over a three-year period. Industrial projects also include a new factory for Philip Morris in Prague. The practice has designed a number of sports complexes in London and throughout the U.K. Retail clients include Mujirushi Ryohin (Muji in Covent Garden, and twelve additional shops due to open in the U.K. and Europe), Liberty plc, Reiss Retail Ltd, and Ted Baker.

Michael Hopkins & Partners was formed in 1976. The practice has five partners: Michael Hopkins (b. 1935), Patricia Hopkins (b. 1942), John Pringle (b. 1951), Ian Sharratt (b. 1948), and Bill Taylor (b. 1957). Michael Hopkins CBE, RA, is a Commissioner with the Royal Fine Art Commission and a member of the RIBA Council. Both he and his wife, Patricia, trained at the Architectural Association, and he was a partner with Foster Associates from 1969 to 1975. In 1994 the couple won the RIBA Gold Medal for Architecture. The practice has designed many successful buildings, including the Hopkins family home in Hampstead, a Greene King brewery in Bury St Edmunds, the Schlumberger Research Laboratories in Cambridge, the Solid State Logic research, development and production building near Oxford, a cutlery factory for David Mellor at Hathersage in West Derbyshire, the Mound Stand at Lord's Cricket Ground, the Bracken House redevelopment in the City of London, and the remodelled Glyndebourne Opera House. Projects in progress include the Bedfont Lakes business park near Heathrow Airport; the Younger University brewery sites; the redevelopment of Melbury House in Marylebone; a new underground station and interchange for the London Underground at Tottenham Court Road; a new Inland Revenue Centre at Nottingham; and new parliamentary offices and anciliary accommodation for the House of Commons, adjoining the Palace of Westminster. The practice serves as consulting architect to the Trustees of the Victoria and Albert Museum and has been appointed to carry out a masterplan for the reorganisation of the 600,000-square-foot listed building on its twelve-acre site in South Kensington (1986). The architects' work was the subject of the BBC documentary 'Designs on Europe', and was exhibited at the Fifth Venice Biennale of Architecture held in 1991.

Richard Horden was born in 1944 and trained at the Architectural Association. He worked with the Farrell Grimshaw Partnership (1971–72), Spence and Webster (1972–74), and Foster Associates (1974–84) before setting up **Richard Horden Associates** in 1985. During this period he was involved with some of the major high-tech projects, including the Sainsbury Centre for the Visual Arts, the Hong Kong and Shanghai Banking Corporation, and Stansted Airport, for Foster Associates. The practice has won a number of international competitions, including, in 1993, one for a 100 metre-high aerodynamic Wing Tower to be sited in the centre of Glasgow; it was also among the three finalists in a competition for a site adjacent to Sydney Harbour. Projects are wide-ranging (a dining hall at Bryanston School, homes for artists and craftsmen in Dorset; and the 'Point Lookout' beach rig and lifesavers' platform, now located at a number of sites in Australia). Private homes such as the Yacht House and the Swiss 'Ski Haus' show the direct inspiration of sailing yachts and of working with aerospace and yachtrig engineers. Major recent projects include a new office tower in Victoria, London; the award-winning Queen's Stand for the Epsom Derby; and a new building for Shell at their headquarters on the Strand, London. Horden has extensive teaching links with universities in Europe, the USA, and Australia.

Howell Killick Partridge & Amis (known as HKPA) was established in 1959 and currently maintains offices in London and Plymouth. The practice is headed by John Partridge, a founding partner, and Roy Murphy and Patrick Lawlor. John Partridge CBE (b. 1924), studied at the Polytechnic School of Architecture, qualifying in 1951. He went on to teach at the Architectural Association and has since served as an assessor for RIBA and Civic Trust Awards and as an external examiner for many colleges in the U.K. He was

elected a Royal Academician in 1980. Major projects for which Partridge was the lead partner include the Wolfson Rayne and Gatehouse building at St Anne's College at Oxford University; the New Hall and Common Room of Saint Antony's College at Oxford University; Wells Hall at the University of Reading; Middlesex Polytechnic's (now Middlesex University) Faculty of Art at Cat Hill; Medway Magistrates' Court; The Albany Theatre and Community Centre, Deptford; the Hall of Justice in Trinidad and Tobago; the Crown courthouses at Warrington, Basildon, and Haywards Heath; and the Chaucer College at the University of Kent at Canterbury, for the Shumei Gakuen Foundation in Tokyo.

Donald W. Insall and Associates is a firm of architects and planning consultants that specialises in the conservation and adaptation of historic buildings and of new buildings in sensitive areas. Established in 1958, the practice has offices in London, Canterbury, and Shrewsbury. The firm's work at the colleges of Cambridge University includes the conservation and improvement of new buildings at Trinity over a period of twenty-five years; repairs and improvements at Jesus and Magdalene; refurbishments and improvements at Queens, Peterhouse, and Gonville & Caius. Major buildings for which the practice has been responsible include the Mansion House and the House of Lords' ceiling in London; Goldsmiths' Hall in the City of London; Speke Hall in Liverpool; Battle Abbey in Sussex; and Raby Castle near Durham. Following the fire at Windsor Castle in 1992, the architects were appointed to coordinate reconstruction work. The firm has served as architectural consultant to Knebworth House since 1970 and has received a number of European Architectural Heritage and Europa Nostra awards and, within the U.K., awards from bodies such as the Civic Trust and RIBA.

Sir Geoffrey Jellicoe, CBE RA was born in 1900 and trained at the Architectural Association in London. His first practice was with J.C. Shepherd, with whom he wrote *Italian Gardens of the Renaissance* in 1925. He set up his own practice in 1931 and collaborated with Russell Page, a firm specialising in gardens for stately homes, until 1939. After the Second World War the practice expanded into town planning,

architecture, and public landscaping, taking on various partners. Since his retirement in 1973, Sir Geoffrey Jellicoe's practice in international landscape projects has developed considerably, and he has continued to design gardens in many countries, including the USA, Britain, and Egypt. Since his eightieth birthday Jellicoe has designed at least a dozen garden projects in the UK alone, including Sutton Place in Surrey and the Shute House garden, with a pool and boating lake, in Wiltshire. He is currently designing the Moody Gardens in Galveston, Texas, a thirty-acre site within a large educational project (to be completed in 1988), and a garden relating to the history of Atlanta, Georgia, for the Historical Society, due for completion in 1996. He was elected a Royal Academician in 1991, is founder and honorary president of the International Federation of Landscape Architects, and has received many awards from the British Landscape Institute, the American Society of Landscape Architects, and the Australian Landscape Institute.

Jestico + Whiles Architects was established in 1977 and has offices in London, Glasgow, and Prague. The principals are Tom Jestico, John Whiles, Robert Collingwood, and Tony Ingram. Early industrial projects at Epsom and Waltham Cross employed lightweight structures and technologies derived from manufacturing. Projects such as Bruges Place, Hawgood Street, and Carlow Street, all in London, combined work spaces, industrial units, and residential areas. The firm has also designed a number of low-energy work spaces for clients such as Friends of the Earth and undertaken the refurbishment of the Policy Studies Institute. The largest project to date is Burrell's Wharf in London Docklands. Other recent projects include a business park in Scotland, several designs for inner-city regeneration, and housing association projects in London. Robert Collingwood is responsible for establishing and running the practice's activities in Central and Eastern Europe. Completed projects in Prague include new offices for the British Council (1990), high-technology offices for Unisys, and the refurbishment and conservation of Ericsson Palace. The practice is also reconstructing Prague's medieval marketplace site, which incorporates the Granowski Palace. In the Slovak

Republic completed projects include the British Council headquarters and a residence for the chargé d'affaires of the British Embassy in Bratislava. In Latvia the British Embassy and Ambassador's residence in Riga are nearing completion.

Eva Jiricna Architects is a London-based practice headed by Eva Jiricna. Born in 1938 in Prague, she qualified as an architect and engineer at the University of Prague in 1963. After arriving in London in 1968, she worked at the Greater London Council (GLC) before joining the Louis de Soissons Partnership in 1969 to work on the Brighton Marina project. Jiricna went into partnership with David Hodges in 1978 and later was commissioned by Richard Rogers Partnership to work on some of the interiors for the new Lloyd's headquarters building in the City of London. In 1985 she won a commission to refurbish the Way-In department at Harrods and formed her own practice with designer Kathy Kerr. The practice was reconstituted as Eva Jiricna Architects in 1986. Jiricna's reputation for interior design work was established by the range of boutiques, restaurants, and coffee bars she created for Joseph, and by other projects, including shoe shops for Joan and David, retail system designs for Vitra GmbH, and several award-winning competition schemes. In 1992, long-standing colleague Jon Tollit (who trained at Leicester Polytechnic) became a fellow director. Recent projects include office interiors for Jardine Insurance in London; the redesign of Brown's, a private club in London; a new Bergdorf Goodman retail outlet in New York; salons in Germany for Vidal Sassoon; and a new gallery and exhibition display design for the Sir John Soane's Museum in London. Eva Jiricna is a member of RIBA and the Architectural Association's governing councils and in 1991 was made a Royal Designer for Industry by the Royal Society of Arts. She lectures frequently and regularly judges international competitions. In 1993 President Vaclav Havel of the Czech Republic invited her to become a member of the Prague Presidential Council. The work of the practice has been featured in a number of books and television programmes.

Ben Johnson is an artist whose sole subject matter for the last twenty-two years has been architecture. His paintings are not perspectives or architectural illustrations but rather celebrations of architectural form, particularly of structure, painted by an outsider 'taking an objective view of a world that fascinates me'. Johnson was born in 1946 and studied at the Royal College of Art. His first solo exhibition was held at the Wickesham Gallery in New York, and subsequent one-person shows have been held at the Institute of Contemporary Art in London, the Fischer Fine Art Gallery, the Royal College of Art (in the exhibition *The Great Engineers*), RIBA (*Painting beyond Architecture – Independent Observation*), the Louis K. Meisel Gallery in New York, and at Arup Associates (*Collaborations: Collaborative Sculpture Projects with Ove Arup and Partners, Arup Associates and Foster Associates*). Johnson has shown in numerous group exhibitions held in London, Edinburgh, Cologne, at the Venice Biennale (1991, photographic collaboration with Sir Norman Foster), New York, Paris, Bordeaux, Lausanne, Seville, Madrid, and Sydney. His corporate clients include IBM U.K. Ltd, British Steel, Cable & Wireless, Volvo (Sweden), Elementa, and British Gas, and his work is owned by public collections in London, Glasgow, Manchester, Paris, and Rotterdam. He is currently working on a painting based on Frank Lloyd Wright's interior of the Rookery Building in Chicago, creating a cityscape of Hong Kong, and preparing for an exhibition in the year 2000, which will take a global look at architecture in cities.

JSP Architects was established in the late 1960s. In its current form the firm has two partners, Michael Stiff and Andrew Trevillion, with offices in London and Berlin. Michael Stiff (b. 1956) and Andrew Trevillion (b. 1954) both trained as architects at the University of Westminster. In 1982 they formed Stiff and Trevillion, which was merged with JSP Architects in 1984. In 1991 a joint venture between JSP and a German practice, CST Architekten, was set up to build a 25,000 square-metre headquarters building for Siemens in Berlin. Stiff has taught at the University of North London, exhibited in a number of touring exhibitions, and shown his drawings in numerous one-man exhibitions held at the Holland Gallery in London. Major built projects include Knaves Beech Business Centres, a twenty-acre site in Buckinghamshire; the refurbishment and extension of Warwick Road in London; Café Kensington in London; The Highway in London, an office building; the Wagamama noodle bar in London; and the Siemens headquarters in Berlin.

Andrew D. King was born in 1967 and is currently a postgraduate student in architecture. He graduated in architecture from the University of Liverpool in 1991 and in 1992 won Bovis/*Architects' Journal* Award for Architecture for his worm's eye axonometric of Salisbury Cathedral, exhibited at that year's Royal Academy Summer Exhibition. He worked for CZWG Architects during his year out (1988–89), working principally on the Radio City development at White City, London and since 1991 has built on his experience with Avery Associates and Jestico + Whiles. While at Avery he was involved with projects such as the National Film Theatre bookshop on London's South Bank. He is currently working at Pascall + Watson on the design of a new check-in extension to South Terminal at Gatwick Airport. His entry to the 1993 Bovis/*Architects' Journal* Award for Architecture for architecture students was shown at Albert Dock in Liverpool, as part of the VisionFest Exhibition.

MacCormac Jamieson Prichard is a London-based architectural practice founded in 1972 by Richard MacCormac, Peter Jamieson, and David Prichard. MacCormac (b. 1938) and Jamieson (b. 1939) both trained at Cambridge University and at University College London. From 1991 to 1993 MacCormac, a Royal Academician elected in 1993, was president of RIBA. He was made a CBE in 1993. Prichard trained at the Bartlett School of Architecture and Planning, University College in London. The work of the practice encompasses a broad range of building types, including university, office, and public buildings; public and private housing; and large commercial projects such as the redevelopment of Spitalfields Market in London, as well as masterplans and designs for urban sites such as Paternoster Square, King's Cross, and London Docklands, and at new towns throughout the U.K. Award-winning projects include the Sainsbury Building at Worcester College, Cambridge University; Niccol theatre/community centre, Cirencester; New Court, Fitzwilliam College, Cambridge University; County Council offices in Havant; and Blue Bear Court, Trinity College, Cambridge University. In 1992 the practice won a competition to design new buildings for Balliol College, Oxford University, and has subsequently completed new buildings for Saint John's College, Oxford University; and Trinity Hall and King's College Library, both at Cambridge University. Projects in progress include the Ruskin Library and a further library extension at Lancaster University; new residences at Balliol College, Oxford University; a new station at Southwark in London for the Jubilee Underground Line extension; and housing association projects in London. All three partners are involved with teaching architecture. Richard MacCormac has written extensively and presents lectures at schools of architecture and other institutions in the U.K. and abroad.

Lucy Malein was born in 1966 and trained at Cambridge University, qualifying as an architect in 1993. Between 1987 and 1991 she worked for Lynn Davis Architects and Clerici Barry Architects in London; Palmer and Turner Architects in Hong Kong; and Berman Gueddes in Oxford, with her year out spent working with Charles Correa Architects in Bombay and Bangalore, on projects such as the British Council building in New Delhi; the Institute of Astrophysics in Pune, India; and the Indian Mission for the U.N. in New York. From 1991 to 1993 she worked for Harrods, Architects Department, which maintains a number of listed buildings. Since 1993 she has been working for Chapman Taylor Architects and has been involved principally with the competition for the refurbishment of the Forum des Halles in Paris and with the feasibility team for European projects. Malein is a founding member of ORANGE, a group of young architects exploring contemporary themes of continuity and process as part of the reinvention of the city for the Millennium.

Leonard Manasseh Partnership was founded in 1950 after the architect Leonard Manasseh won a competition for the 1951 Festival of Britain. Manasseh CBE RA, trained at the Architectural Association, of which he is a past President. He has also been President of the Franco-British Union of Architects and is currently President of the Royal West of England Academy. He was elected a Royal Academician in

1976. Partner Ian Baker also trained at the Architectural Association and joined the practice in 1954. The practice's award-winning projects include Wellington County Park, which incorporates the National Dairy Museum; the National Motor Museum in Beaulieu, Hampshire; King's Lynn Magistrates and Crown Courts; housing for the elderly in Basildon; and offices for Rotork Engineering in Bath. Recent work includes an office, residential, and hotel development for the Royal Hotel site in Bristol; a shopping centre and pedestrian arcades at Liverpool Central Station; the replanning of the Old Royal Observatory at Greenwich; planning schemes at Eastbourne; and Glensanda coastal quarry in Scotland; the summit of Mount Snowdon in Wales, and the historic centre of King's Lynn. As executive architects under the direction of the British Museum, the practice has undertaken the refurbishment of the museum's Edward VII Galleries.

David Marks and Julia Barfield Architects was founded in 1987. David Marks (b. 1952) trained at the Architectural Association and worked for Richard Rogers Partnership for seven years. He was responsible for a major part of the Lloyd's headquarters building in the City of London. Julia Barfield trained at the Architectural Association and between 1982 and 1988 worked for Foster Associates on projects such as the Renault Centre in Swindon; the BBC headquarters in London; and the Royal Academy of Arts' Sackler Galleries, for which she was project architect. Prior to that she worked for Richard Rogers Partnership on the Inmos micro-processor factory at Newport in South Wales. The team's chief projects to date include £36 million of central facilities at a business park for Speyhawk in Reading; an office development at King's Cross Marina in London and masterplans for various dockyard development projects in France, Sweden, and Scotland. The practice has designed two prize-winning Olympic stadia for Berlin 2000. Projects in progress include a £1 million water-sports activities centre at Queen's Dock in Liverpool and a £12 million extension to the North Terminal at Gatwick Airport.

Eric Parry Associates was founded by Eric Parry, who trained at the Royal College of Art and at the Architectural Association. He subsequently taught

urban design at the Architectural Association and, since 1983, at Cambridge University. His buildings and interiors include artists' studios for Tom Phillips and Antony Gormley; an office building at Stockley Park; the headquarters of Stanhope Properties plc; the club building at the Chiswick Park development; a house for developer Stuart Lipton; a house in the Fens in Cambridgeshire; and the Château de Paulin in France. Collegiate work, unbuilt but pending, includes three houses for graduate accommodation for Corpus Christi College and for Pembroke College, both at Cambridge University. The practice was incorporated in 1991 when Nello Gregori and Philip Meadowcroft joined as co-directors. Joint projects, at a range of scales, include bars for the Ministry of Sound nightclub in London, the first Master's Lodge in Cambridge, and the masterplan for a new General and District Hospital for Norfolk and Norwich.

Powell Moya Partnership was established in 1946 by Sir Philip Powell CBE and Hidalgo Moya and is currently run by nine directors, of which five are shareholders. Sir Philip Powell was born in 1921 and trained at the Architectural Association. The practice designed many notable housing and educational projects during its early days, gaining prominence for the Skylon tower designed for the Festival of Britain in 1951 as the result of a competition. Sir Philip has won numerous medals and awards for his architectural work, including the Royal Gold Medal for Architecture in 1974, and he was elected a Royal Academician in 1972. Among Powell and Moya's principal projects are extensions to Brasenose College and to Corpus Christi College, both at Oxford University; and the Cripps Building for Saint John's College at Cambridge University; the Chichester Festival Theatre; the Museum of London; the Queen Elizabeth II Conference Centre in London; the masterplan and faculty, residential, and new university library buildings for the Royal Holloway and Bedford New College of the University of London; the redevelopment of the Great Ormond Street Hospital for Sick Children; and the Wansbeck low-energy hospital in Northumberland. Recent competition entries include the European Parliament Building in Strasbourg. Projects in progress include a masterplan for Brunswick

Wharf/East India Dock Basin in London Docklands.

Reid Pinney Architects was established in 1985, when architect Richard Reid (b. 1939) won first prize in the international competition for the Cherry Garden Pier Housing in London and in the competition for new civic offices for Epping Forest, a project that won a RIBA award in 1991. He has worked as an architect for Building Design Partnership and as Senior Planning Officer at the Corporation of London, and has taught architecture at University College, Dublin, and at the Polytechnic of the South Bank since 1965. His publications include the *Guides* to Great Britain, Scotland, and Ireland (Robert Nicholson) and *The Book of Buildings* (Michael Joseph). Mark Pinney (b. 1957) trained at the Polytechnic of the South Bank and has worked for Trevor Dannatt and Partners and for Michael Percival. The practice has specialised in mixed-use housing projects and urban design, and the architects are at present urban design consultants for the Cardiff Bay Development Corporation in Wales, and for the City of Leipzig (following a competition win for the masterplan of the 160-acre district of Kleinzschocher). In 1992 they won first prize in a competition for mixed-use housing and, commercial scheme for a four-acre site on the edge of the city of Leipzig. Recent projects include a 500-bed hospital in Saudi Arabia; conservation and design work at the Temple Cobham in Kent; and the design of Greenville for the Urban Village Company. The work of the practice has been exhibited at a number of venues in the U.K. and abroad.

Richard Rogers was born in Florence in 1933. After moving to London in 1938, he studied at the Architectural Association and at Yale University, on a Fulbright Scholarship. In 1963 he established Team 4 with his wife, Su Rogers, and with Norman Foster and Wendy Foster. In 1970 he founded Piano + Rogers with the Italian architect Renzo Piano, and the practice went on to win a competition for the Centre National d'Art et Culture Georges Pompidou in Paris. In 1977 **Richard Rogers Partnership** was founded with John Young, Marco Goldschmied, and Mike Davies. The next year the practice won a limited competition to design the now world-famous Lloyd's building in the City of London. Other award-winning projects designed subsequently include the Inmos microprocessor factory at Newport in South Wales; PA Technology, Princeton, New Jersey; the restoration and conversion of the Billingsgate Fish Market in London into a dealing room for Citibank; Magasin d'Usine, a commercial centre in Nantes, France; and offices at Thames Wharf. More recently the practice has undertaken master– planning, building an extension to the Marseilles airport in France, and has designed the new greenfield site headquarters for Lloyd's Register of Shipping, the European Court of Human Rights in Strasbourg, and the Rover Building in Iikura, Tokyo. Locations for recent master-planning projects include Potsdamer Platz in Berlin and the new Lu Jia Zui business district of Shanghai. The practice, which has offices in London, Berlin, and Tokyo, has recently been commissioned to design law courts in Bordeaux, and three blocks on the Daimler-Benz site in Berlin master-planned by Renzo Piano. In London the firm is currently completing the new headquarters building for Channel 4 and is working on designs for Heathrow Airport's new Terminal 5 as well as modifications to Terminal 1. Richard Rogers's recent book, *A New London* (Penguin, 1992), conveys his concern for the environment and the regeneration of the public realm. He was elected a Royal Academician in 1978, received the Gold Medal for Architecture from RIBA in 1985, and was made Chevalier de l'Ordre National de la Légion d'Honneur in 1986. Chairman of the Architecture Foundation and the Building Experiences Trust in London, Rogers was knighted for services to architecture in 1991.

Peter Salter was born in 1947 and trained at the Architectural Association. His professional experience includes work for the London Boroughs of Hammersmith, Ealing, and Lambeth, and with architects Robin Clayto, Bone & Morris, and Peter and Alison Smithson. In 1980 he began teaching at the Architectural Association and in 1989 became Unit Master in the Diploma School there. From 1987 to 1989 he directed the technical studies component of the school's landscaping course. He has also taught architecture at Cambridge University and many other architectural schools and institutions in the U.K. and abroad. In 1982 he founded the architectural practice CODA with Chris Macdonald and Ingrid Morris. They submitted entries for competitions for projects, among them the University of Durham's Oriental Museum, the Venice Biennale Accademia Bridge, and the IBA in Berlin. Built projects include a folly at the 1990 Osaka Expo in Japan, a mountain pavilion at Kamiichi, and a museum of wood carving at Inami. Salter's proposal for a Thai fish restaurant, drawings of which were shown at the Royal Academy, won an Bovis/*Architects' Journal* Award. Macdonald & Salter, as the practice has become known, has exhibited work at the Architectural Association, at the Heinz Gallery in London, the Architectural Centre in Dublin, the Storefront Gallery in New York, Bennington College in Vermont, and the GA Gallery in Tokyo.

Michael Sandle is an artist. He was born in 1936 and studied at the Douglas School of Art and Technology on the Isle of Man before moving to London to study printmaking at the Slade School of Fine Art at the University of London. In 1959 he travelled throughout Europe, and in 1960 he went to work as a lithographer in Paris for Atelier Patris. Later that year he moved back to England and formed a working association with Christina Bertoni, Laurence Burt, Michael Chilton, Tom Hudson, and Terry Setch, together referred to as the Leicester Group. After some years of teaching at Coventry College of Art and at the Slade School, Sandle moved to Canada, where he was made Visiting Associate Professor at the University of Calgary, Alberta, and at the University of Victoria, British Columbia. In 1973 he moved to Germany, where he taught sculpture at the Fachhochschule für Gestaltung in Pforzheim, becoming Professor of Sculpture in 1977. In 1980 he was made Professor at the Akademie der Bildenden Künste in Karlsruhe, a post he currently holds. Sandle has exhibited his work internationally since 1958. In 1988 a major retrospective of his sculpture and drawings was shown at the Whitechapel Art Gallery in London and the Württembergischer Kunstverein in Stuttgart. Since this date one-man shows have been held at the Ernst Museum in Budapest and at OPS in Lodz in Poland, both organised by the British Council. In 1988 Sandle completed *Saint George and the Dragon*, a bronze sculpture for the Mountleigh

Group plc in London. From 1988 to 1992 he worked on the project for the memorial to the siege of Malta, installed in Valletta in Malta. He has shown work most recently at the Angel Row Gallery in Nottingham (1992) and as part of the exhibition *Kunst der Neunziger Jahre* held at the Badischer Kunstverein in Karlsruhe (1993). Sandle's work can be found in a number of public collections internationally. He was elected a Royal Academician in 1982.

John Simpson & Partners was established in 1980. Its interests and expertise lie in the area of classical and traditional architecture and in urban planning and design. John Simpson (b. 1954) studied at the Bartlett School of Architecture and Planning at the University of London. His major projects include the masterplan for the redevelopment of Paternoster Square and the area surrounding Saint Paul's Cathedral in the City of London, and London Bridge City, another sensitive urban site seven acres in size on the banks of the River Thames opposite the Tower of London. Simpson's proposals for Upper Donnington, a new village in Berkshire, sought to re-establish within the context of the English countryside the idea of freestanding settlements of mixed use and mixed community. Current work being carried out by the practice includes a number of urban and rural villages such as the extension of Aylesbury and the plan for Dickens New Heath Village for Solihull Metropolitan Borough Council outside Birmingham. Simpson has also designed the masterplan for Pentire Development at Newquay for the Duchy of Cornwall and is designing the new market building for the first 1994 phase of the Duchy's Poundbury development at Dorchester. Other works include a number of new buildings for clients in the City of London, various country houses such as the Ashfold House in Sussex, and a new house for the King and Queen of Jordan at Ascot in Berkshire. Simpson has also designed furniture.

Neil Southard is an architect (b. 1964) who trained at the Chelsea School of Art and the Royal College of Art. He is currently working for Richard Rogers Partnership. He has won various awards and lectures frequently. **Alex Ritchie** (b. 1962) trained at Glasgow College of Design and Manchester Polytechnic. He is currently head of the Environmental Design department

at Imagination Ltd, the London design consultancy. He frequently lectures and tutors. **Ian MacDuff** studied architecture at the University of Cape Town. He has taught design in Sydney and in Cape Town and currently works for Sir Norman Foster and Partners' Hong Kong office. The three architects began working on the masterplan for London's South Bank Centre in 1987, which led to their strong interest in the Festival of Britain and the resulting exhibition that opened at RIBA to mark the fortieth anniversary of the 1951 event. Southard and Ritchie are preparing *The Thames Millennium*, a further exhibition focussing on twenty-two sites on and around the river Thames, with the aim of provoking discussion about civic regeneration throughout the U.K. **Henrietta Cooper** is a freelance graphic designer and independent consultant working in print and exhibition design. She trained at Central Saint Martins and won an award for retail design from the Royal Society of Arts in London in 1989.

James Stirling Michael Wilford and Associates was established in 1971 by James Stirling and Michael Wilford. Stirling was born in Glasgow in 1926 and studied architecture at the University of Liverpool and urban planning in London. Wilford was born in Surbiton in 1938 and studied at the Northern Polytechnic School of Architecture. Stirling began working in private practice in 1956 with James Gowan and remained until 1963 when he began to work solo. Wilford, who had joined the practice in 1960, became his senior assistant, and later associate partner, before they joined forces. Two projects brought Stirling acclaim early in his career: Leicester University's Engineering Building (1958–63, designed with James Gowan), and the History Faculty Library at Cambridge University (1967–68). In 1977 the firm won a major limited competition for the new Staatsgalerie in Stuttgart, Germany, which led to many commissions for cultural buildings, including the Sackler Museum at Harvard University in Cambridge, Mass., the Wissenschaftszentrum in Berlin, the Clore Gallery extension to the Tate Gallery in London, the Tate Gallery in Liverpool, and the Performing Arts Centre at Cornell University in Ithaca, N.Y. More recently the practice has completed two projects in Germany, a music school and theatre academy in Stuttgart and the headquarters for B. Braun at Mel-

sungen, in addition to the Library at the University of California at Irvine, a stadium development in Seville, and Temasek Polytechnic in Singapore. During the course of his career James Stirling lectured internationally and received many awards, including the RIBA Gold Medal for Architecture, the Pritzker Prize, and the Praemium Imperiale Award. His untimely death in June 1992, just twelve days after he was knighted, prompted countless international tributes. Widely regarded as one of the most original and influential architects of his generation, Stirling left a distinguished legacy of buildings. Michael Wilford continues his practice as Michael Wilford and Partners (incorporating James Stirling Michael Wilford and Partners). The firm's current projects include the Philharmonic Hall in Los Angeles and the Kyoto Centre in Japan.

Quinlan Terry was born in London in 1937 and trained at the Architectural Association. In 1962 he joined Raymond Erith in practice and for the next eleven years they worked together on buildings designed in the classical tradition, among them Kingswalden, Hertfordshire; the new Common Room Building at Gray's Inn in London; Saint Mary's Church, Paddington Green (which they restored); and a large temple in the Middle East. After Erith's death in 1973 Terry maintained his adherence to classicism, evident in his recent stone and brick country houses for private clients that include Waverton House, Gloucestershire; Fawley House, Henley on Thames, Berkshire; Newfield House, Ripon, Yorkshire; Pinoak Farm in Kentucky; and six private villas in Regent's Park for the Crown Estate Commissioners. Terry's commercial schemes include offices and flats in Soho, and offices, shops, flats, car parks, and landscaping at Richmond Riverside. His public buildings include the new Lecture Theatre, Maitland Robinson Library, and Junior Common Room at Downing College, Cambridge University, and the new Brentwood Cathedral in Essex. He has undertaken landscaping at West Green for Lord McAlpine and at Thenford for Michael Heseltine, the Conservative MP, and refurbishment and restoration work at Queen's College Chapel, Oxford University, and in the state drawing rooms of the Prime Minister's London residence at number 10 Downing Street in Whitehall, London.

Troughton McAslan was formed in 1983 by Jamie Troughton and John McAslan. Jamie Troughton studied at Cambridge University and subsequently worked for Foster Associates and Richard Rogers Partnership. John McAslan attended Edinburgh University and after two years with Cambridge Seven Associates in Boston, Mass., he also went to work for Richard Rogers Partnership. The practice's early work consisted of award-winning studio and office refurbishments in London, notably the Design House in Camden Town. Small-scale residential projects and competition-winning entries followed, leading to a number of technologically advanced new-build and conversion projects. In 1989 and 1991 a two-phased European headquarters building for Apple Computer was completed at Stockley Park, also designed by the practice, with interior and landscaping. Further commercial buildings completed include those for London Merchant Securities, Great Portland Estates, Olympia & York, and a new station for British Rail at Red Hill, Surrey, which won the International Brunel Award. Educational institutions and museum buildings include a prize-winning new college in Kobe, Japan, for Saint Catherine's College, Oxford University (1991), and master–plan proposals in 1993 for the Cincinnati Art Museum in Ohio. The office is currently involved in a number of masterplanning, new-build, and restoration projects, some in sensitive urban-conservation settings. These include the London Underground's Operational Centre at Acton, West London; transport schemes for the Jubilee Line Extension, CrossRail, and for the city of Bangkok, Thailand; transport interchanges in London, Doncaster, and Edinburgh; and restoration of some landmark twentieth-century buildings in England, continental Europe, and the USA, notably the Grade One listed De La Warr Pavilion at Bexhill-on-Sea.

Colin St John Wilson was born in Cheltenham in 1922 and studied at Cambridge University and at University College in London. During the first half of the 1950s he worked for the Housing Division of the London County Council's Architects' Department designing prototype housing, and from 1956 to 1964 he headed a private practice in Cambridge in association with Sir Leslie Martin. In 1965 he established **Colin St John Wilson and Partners** in Cambridge; since 1969 the practice has been based in London and directed by the architect along with three partners, John Collier, M. J. Long, and John Horner. From 1975 to 1989 he was Professor and Head of the Department of Architecture at Cambridge University. He has also been visiting critic at Yale University's School of Architecture and Visiting Professor at the Massachussetts Institute of Technology (M.I.T.) in Cambridge, Mass., and has lectured and taught internationally. His principal buildings include Harvey Court at Gonville and Caius and the Stone Building at Peterhouse (with Sir Leslie Martin), both at Cambridge University; extensions to the School of Architecture at Cambridge University and to the British Museum in London; the Biochemistry Laboratory for the Agricultural Research Council; private houses in Cambridge; and a number of libraries, including the library at Queen Mary College, University of London; the Bishop Wilson Memorial Library in Springfield, Essex; and the Chicago Public Library (in association with executive architects Beeby, Babka). The practice began work on the new British Library at St Pancras in London in 1975, with a brief to incorporate all the facilities of the reference centre of the library on one site. A further period of work to 'complete' the project at the size of phase one of the original three-phase design was commenced in 1988, and construction began in 1992. Wilson has written numerous articles for the architectural press, and in 1992 he published a book of selected writings entitled *Architectural Reflections* (Butterworth and Heinemann). He was elected a Royal Academician in 1990 and is a member of the Board of the Arts Council and Chairman of its Architecture Unit, a member of the Council of the Royal Academy of Arts, and Commander of the Order of the Lion of Finland.

Zoe Zenghelis was born in Athens, Greece, in 1938, and studied stage design and painting at Regent Street Polytechnic in London. In 1975 she founded the Office for Metropolitan Architecture (OMA) with the Dutch architect Rem Koolhaas, the Dutch painter Madelon Vriesendorp, and the architect Elia Zenghelis. Since 1984 she has directed the Colour Workshop at the Architectural Association and has taught at architectural schools in England, Scotland, and the USA. She has exhibited at numerous venues in London, New York, Paris, and Athens. Her architectural paintings in particular have been widely published and have been shown at the 1980 Venice Biennale; in the Time-Life Building, New York; The Museum of Modern Art in New York; the Städelschule in Frankfurt; the Nationalgalerie in Berlin; the Gemeentemuseum in The Hague; the Max Protetch Gallery in New York; and the Stedelijk Museum in Amsterdam.